International studies in the history of sport
series editor J. A. Mangan

Sport, politics and communism

For Sean and Perry

Sport, politics and communism

James Riordan

MANCHESTER UNIVERSITY PRESS

Manchester and New York

Distributed exclusively in the USA and Canada by St. Martin's Press

Copyright © James Riordan 1991   *9100016665*

Published by Manchester University Press
Oxford Road, Manchester M13 9PL, UK, England
and Room 400, 175 Fifth Avenue, New York, NY 10010, USA

Distributed exclusively in the USA and Canada
by St. Martin's Press, Inc., 175 Fifth Avenue, New York, NY 10010, USA

British Library cataloguing in publication data
Riordan, James 1936–
    Sport, politics and communism. – (International studies in
    the history of sport : 0955–8284).
    1. Communist countries. Sports
    I. Title   II. Series
    796.091717

American Library of Congress cataloging in publication data
Riordan, James, 1936–
    Sport, politics and communism / James Riordan.
        p. cm. — (International studies in the history of sport)
    Includes index.
    ISBN 0–7190–2850–7
    1. Sports and state—Europe, Eastern.   I. Title.   II. Series.
    GV706–35.R46   1991
    796'.0947—dc20   90–25265

ISBN 0 7190 2850 7 *hardback*

Photoset in Linotron Palatino
by Northern Phototypesetting Company Limited, Bolton
Printed in Great Britain
by Billings Ltd., Worcester

Contents

Series editor's introduction

This series was launched, as its title suggests, on the premise that it would explore the political, cultural, social and economic aspects of sport *internationally*.

Recent volumes in the series have dealt with capitalist communities. James Riordan redresses the balance with this consideration of the politics of sport in communist societies.

As Riordan makes clear, in many communist states sport has been at the centre, not the periphery of politics (and society). It has proved to be a far from marginal phenomenon in the history of communism. It has served as a basic form of social control highlighting 'the custodial role of the state, the power to shape and control the lives of its citizens'. Far from being an instrument of political altruism bringing the pleasure of involvement, active and passive, to all, it has been too frequently an instrument of conformist coercion.

Nevertheless, Riordan is undoubtedly right to warn against the prospect of an athletic millennium as nation after nation rejects communism and adopts capitalism. Different political ideologies can easily offer opportunities for the same (and other) abuses as characterised sport under communism.

While Riordan is tentative in his prognostications for the future, he is firm in his final assertion. No doubt the fate of present political reforms will be decided by means of the politburo, polling station or perhaps (God forbid) the battlefield rather than the playing field, but the ultimate shape of sport in former communist countries *will* tell us a great deal 'about the failure and success of the socialist experiment'.

In fact, although Riordan modestly omits to say so, his book already does this!

J. A. Mangan

Preface
Sport and communism in the light of East European revolutions

Such is the disorienting pace of change in the communist world, notably in Eastern Europe,[1] that communism and communist sport have come to possess quite a new meaning since the momentous events of late 1989. It is no longer evident – if it ever was – what communism or socialism, communist or socialist sport signify, or how exactly they may be contrasted with capitalism or capitalist sport. Somehow it seemed simpler to be confronted by the old distinctions: communist sport was largely state-directed for utilitarian purposes; capitalist sport was largely not state-directed and was principally guided by the profit motive. Neither were ever that clear-cut, of course. But now even that framework for drawing elementary distinctions has been removed by the transformations initiated by the revolutions of 1989. That year marked a watershed not only in East European history, but in world history too. It was one of the historic moments of modern times, comparable to 1848 and 1917. In one country after another the ruling regime succumbed in the face of massive popular protest. Poland, Hungary, East Germany, Bulgaria, Czechoslovakia and, most dramatically of all, Romania, all saw their Communist Party leaders ousted, a new government installed, and contested elections held. In Albania, Yugoslavia and the USSR, change has been less cataclysmic, yet it is perfectly possible to predict that no East European country will possess a communist regime by the mid-1990s.

Stalinism in Europe is dead (save in Albania), Leninism is in its death throes; even Gorbachevism is apparently too little, too late.

A compelling feature of the turbulent events in Europe's erstwhile communist states has been the intensive debate about sport. Far from being at the periphery of politics, sport has been right at the centre. In Romania, athletes manned the barricades, with Dinamo Club members defending their patrons, the Securitate, in opposition to the army athletes of Steaua whose Olympic gold medalists in shooting were

1

among those firing on the secret police. Romanian rugby captain Florica Murariu and team-mate Radu Dadac were just two of the sports heroes who fell in battle.

In East Germany, sports stars like Katarina Witt, Roland Matthes and Kornelia Ender all complained of having had their homes and cars vandalised by one-time 'fans' angry at the privileges of the stars and their close association with the old regime. The officials of the GDR's umbrella sports organisation, the DTSB, resigned *en masse*; its finance director Franz Rydz drowned himself.

In Hungary, Poland and Czechoslovakia, several clubs hurriedly sought a new name, sponsorship and even Western commercial backing.

Within the Soviet Union, in early 1990 Lithuanian and Georgian teams withdrew from all Soviet cup and league competitions, and several Soviet republics (Latvia, Estonia, Lithuania, Moldavia, Georgia) set up their own Olympic committees which have requested recognition from the International Olympic Committee (IOC). A number of Dinamo clubs have also changed their names – e.g. Dinamo Tbilisi in Georgia became Iveria in 1990.

With the welling up of hostility and revenge directed against the paramilitary forces that have shored up the old corrupt regimes, it is understandable that their sponsored sports clubs should suffer by association. For, as we shall see below, since the end of the Second World War the East European (and world communist) sports system has been dominated by clubs of the security police and the armed forces: Dinamo (Tirana, Bucharest, Berlin, Zagreb, as well as Moscow, Kiev, Minsk and Tbilisi) and the clubs of the armed forces, such as Dukla Liberec in Czechoslovakia, Legia in Poland, TsSKA in Bulgaria and the Soviet Union, Vorwärts in East Germany, Honved in Hungary, Steaua in Romania and Red Star in Yugoslavia.

Such events have demonstrated that sport in such countries has been identified in the popular consciousness with privilege, paramilitary coercion, hypocrisy, distorted priorities and, in the case of the non-Soviet states, with an alien, Soviet-imposed institution. Further, most sports heroes have officially been soldiers or police officers, guardians of public order and role models for a disciplined and obedient citizenry. Future heroes are likely to be civilians, not warriors.

Some in the West have looked with envy at the successful talent-spotting and nurturing system developed in the communist states. It has indeed brought considerable acclaim in world sport – the USSR and GDR have dominated the summer and winter Olympics of recent years (see Chapter 8). Yet many people, East and West of the Oder-Neisse, have abhorred the flag-waving razzmatazz accompanying sporting victories, which were evidently more for the benefit of bringing prestige and recognition to the regime and its ideology than to the people. The elite sports system, moreover, producing medal winners to demonstrate the superiority of communist society, is popularly perceived as being a diversion from the realities of living 'under communism'. As John Hoberman has put it in regard to GDR sport, the events of 1989 were 'a response to the discipline and dehumanizing limitations inflicted on athletes by the requirements of high-performance sport'.[2]

Since Mikhail Gorbachev came to power in 1985, radical changes have appeared in communist sport. The functionalised, bureaucratic mould has been broken. Until then, not only had the Soviet-pioneered, state-controlled system hampered a true appraisal of the realities beneath the 'universal' statistics and the 'idealised' veneer, it had prevented concessions to particular groups in the population. It produced the 'we-know-what's-best-for-you' syndrome, whereby men tell women what sports they should play; the fit tell the disabled that sport is not for them (e.g. Soviet disabled athletes – thirteen blind men – attended the Paralympics for the first time only in 1988); the political leadership, mindful of the nation's and ideology's international reputation, decides that Olympic (i.e. European and North American) sports are the only civilised forms of culture.

In the heat of battle, it is tempting to blame Stalinists and 'stagnators' for neglecting 'sport for all' in their race for glory. In truth, much effort was exerted over the years to involve the public in some form of exercise and recreation that was completely free of charge – whether through the ubiquitous fitness programme, work-based facilities, or compulsory sports lessons for all students in their first years at college. But it was the coercive nature of sporting activities, their being part of the plan-fulfilled system (every school, factory, farm and region received a sports quota and incurred penalties if they fell short) that turned people off. The system only highlighted the custodial role of the state, the power to shape and control the lives of its citizens.

In the case of the non-Soviet nations, there was the added irritant of having to put up with a system tailored by Stalin and imposed from without in contradiction to their own traditions. Sokol gymnastics were banned in Czechoslovakia and Poland after 1948. Youth organisations involved in recreation, like the YMCA, Boy Scouts and the Jewish

Maccabi, were similarly proscribed. Pre-1939 Olympic committees were disbanded by the new regimes, on Moscow's orders, and their members often persecuted – for example, Estonia's two pre-war IOC members, Friedrich Akel and Joakim Puhk, were both executed by the Soviet secret police, the NKVD, in 1940.

All this happened in spite of the long traditions and often superior standards existing in the non-Russian states: Lithuania had won the European basketball championships in 1937 and 1939; Estonia had competed independently in the Olympics between 1920 and 1936, winning six gold, seven silver and nine bronze medals; Germany had pioneered sports medicine since the late nineteenth century.

Being tied to the USSR meant following Soviet foreign policy, including that on Olympic boycotts. The Soviet Party decision to boycott the 1984 Summer Olympics in Los Angeles was simply passed down to other members of the Warsaw Pact – no sports or national Olympic committee, not to mention athletes, were consulted. Romania demurred, though hardly because of player-power.

As we shall see, it was the Soviet state-controlled sports system that was adopted by, or imposed upon (along with other political, social and economic institutions), those countries of Eastern Europe liberated by the Red Army in the period 1945–49. The eight other nations of the Soviet-dominated half of Europe were forced to adopt the Soviet system of state control of sport, sports science and medicine, the national fitness programme (Prepared for Work and Defence), the sports rankings pyramid for each Olympic sport, trade union sports societies, state 'shamateurism' (by which the professional athletes claimed full-time employment as army officers, skilled workers, or full-time students, with appropriate remuneration from outside sport – once the USSR decided to join the Olympic movement in 1951) and overall control by the security forces and the army.

Such was the extent of the Soviet blueprint being copied that very often the Soviet name was retained (however insensitive this may have been to national pride and dignity), as in the case of the KGB's Dinamo clubs, the State Committee on Physical Culture and Sport: *Gosudarstvenny komitet po fizicheskoi kulture i sportu* in the USSR; *Staatssekretariat für Körperkultur und Sport* in the GDR; and the monthly theoretical journal *Theory and Practice of Physical Culture*: *Teoriya i praktika fizicheskoi kultury* in the USSR; *Theorie und Praxis der Körperkultur* in the GDR; *Teorie a Praxe Tělesné Výchovy* in Czechoslovakia, and so on. And whenever the Soviet sports structure altered, that in the rest of Eastern

Europe followed suit. It is hardly surprising, then, that such contempt for national traditions should finally provoke mass anger and hatred expressed so violently in the popular uprisings of late 1989.

The domination of sport by the state for political purposes also resulted in much hypocrisy and chicanery forced upon players and public. There was the above-mentioned falsity of the state professional status by way of an army officer sinecure, eternal studenthood, or false registration at a workplace. Further, evidence is emerging of long-term state production, testing, monitoring and administering of perform-ance-enhancing drugs in regard to young people from the age of 7–8 (see Chapter 7). It is this long-time hypocrisy by members of the ruling regimes – loudly condemning drug abuse in the West as a typical excess of capitalism, while concealing their own involvement in a far more extensive programme of state manufacture and administering of drugs – that has brought into question the state manipulation of sport.

The reports now emerging from the one-time communist states of Eastern Europe are often not so much responses to new orders from above; they are much more the result of a 'revolution from below', on the part of athletes, coaches, journalists and fans, seeking to put an end to decades of false amateurism, state-run drug abuse and bureaucratic control.

The revolutionary changes in Eastern Europe met little response initially from communist leaderships beyond the European continent. Partly this is because some of the poorer communist nations recovering from ruinous wars, in Indochina and Afghanistan, have more immediate priorities than sport and, unlike other developing nations – such as Ethiopia, Mongolia and North Korea – have never attempted to promote an elite sports infrastructure. Elsewhere, China had in any case begun to reorient its sport system in the early 1980s when it started to decentralise and open its doors to Western developers. Not only did this result in Western commercial sponsorship of hitherto neglected recrea-tional pursuits like golf, motor racing and baseball, it also encouraged previously banned sports – boxing for men *and* for women, women's body-building and weight-lifting – for voyeuristic and profit-making purposes based on Western prototypes. Boxing is an interesting example of the change of policy. After the communist take-over of 1949, boxing, which had been introduced to China by Western missionaries at the turn of the century, was prohibited as a sport in that it was said to be at variance with China's traditions of non-bodily-contact sports. It says much for China's frantic desire to seek a way out of its sporting isolation that it preferred to remodel its system on that of the USA rather than of the USSR, even admitting women's boxing from 1987 – a sport palpably at odds with Chinese traditions and values. Much of the volte-face in sport occurred after the 1984 Los Angeles Olympic Games to which China (the only communist nation to take part aside from Romania and Yugoslavia) sent both the largest communist team and a delegation headed by Wei Zhenlan to learn from the Los Angeles Organizing Committee 'how to make sport pay'. Subsequently, Chinese sport policy was said officially to be characterised by five new principles: corporate sponsorship and individual funding (from wealthy overseas Chinese), lottery tickets, tour groups, the sale of advertising rights for international events held in China, and business management of Chinese sports amenities and clubs. Henceforth sport was to be a profit-making institution.[3]

To be fair, China also began in the mid-1980s to pay serious attention in sport to disadvantaged groups in the population – women, the handicapped and ethnic minorities – for all of whom it expanded sports facilities and tournaments. Another motivating factor in the transformation was the desire to abandon the (always half-hearted) 'friendship through sport' policy in order to achieve recognition and prestige through sporting victories and a higher profile through hosting major events, like the Asian Games (1990) and the Olympic Games (bidding for 2000). It has had mixed fortunes in its initial aim of demonstrating supremacy over South-East Asia, having won more gold medals than South Korea and Japan at the 1986 Asian Games, but coming third to both in the 1988 Olympics held in Seoul. But at least by the end of the 1980s Chinese athletes were competing in a wide range of sports all over the world, and the world's top stars were entertaining the Chinese public.

Both North Korea and Cuba in recent years have somewhat isolated themselves from world sport by boycotting the 1984 (Los Angeles) and 1988 (Seoul) Olympics and a number of other world championships. None the less, both have continued their strong commitment to elite sport. The political and economic isolation of the two states has had repercussions in perpetuating rigid political dictatorships and, in sport, using sporting victories to make the rest of the world take note of their existence. Cuba's example is the most arresting: not only have its athletes consistently been placed second to those of the USA in the Pan-American Games, they have improved the country's standing in the Olympic medal table from 58th in 1960 to 8th in 1976 and 4th in 1980.

Fidel Castro has never disguised the political role he sees sport playing in the world: 'Imperialism has tried to humiliate Latin American countries, to instil an inferiority complex in them . . . It has used sport for that purpose.'[4] In that context he sees Cuban Olympic success as 'a sporting, psychological, patriotic and revolutionary victory'.[5] He looks forward to the day when Cuba can prove the superiority of its national sport, baseball, over that of US baseball: 'One day, we shall beat them [the Yankees] at baseball too and then the advantages of revolutionary over capitalist sport will be demonstrated'.[6]

For the poorer communist countries, like Cuba, North Korea and Mongolia, the investment of scarce resources in producing elite athletes has resulted in a grossly distorted scale of priorities, with health, education, housing, nutrition, consumer goods, even 'sport for all', suffering by contrast. It is this stark contrast that is being challenged by popular protest movements all over the communist world.

To return to Eastern Europe, there are those sports enthusiasts there who would, in their haste to escape from the past, clearly like to embrace virtually every aspect of Western sport. Just as those who hanker after an unfettered market economy are often blind to its deficiencies – unemployment, inflation, insecurity, asset-stripping and greed – so those who wish to install unbridled market sport may stumble upon some unexpected problems and lose even more of their national heritage, even 'socialist gains', by throwing out the baby with the bath water. The American writer Robert Edelman has signalled the dangers: 'Removing bureaucrats may be seen as a democratic step. Yet it also creates opportunities for the elitism, special privileges, corruption, illegal gambling, exploitation of athletes, and irresponsibility of organizers associated with big-time professional sport under capitalism.'[7]

Ultimately, the future of East European sport is for the people to decide. At least they are beginning to have a bigger say in shaping that future. We can only wish them well, offering help and opinion should they ask for it. Outside interference has done harm enough already.

Notes

1 Eastern Europe is taken here to include the following nine states: USSR (population 280 million), Poland (37m), Yugoslavia (24m), Romania (23m), the German Democratic Republic (17m), Czechoslovakia (16m), Hungary (11m), Bulgaria (9m) and Albania (3m).

2 John Hoberman, 'The transformation of East German sport', Paper presented at the annual meeting of the American Association for the Advancement of Slavic Studies, Chicago, 4 November 1989, p. 1.

3 Susan Brownell, 'The changing relationship between sport and the state in the People's Republic of China', Paper presented at the conference on *Sport: the Third Millenium*, Quebec City, 21–5 May 1990, p. 3.
4 Fidel Castro, in S. Castanes (ed.), *Fidel. Sobre el deporte* (El Deporte, Havana, 1974), pp. 287–8.
5 Fidel Castro, *El Deporte*, no. 3, 1976, p. 1.
6 Castro, in Castanes, p. 288.
7 Robert Edelman, 'The professionalization of Soviet sport', Unpublished paper, 1990, pp. 21–2.

Chapter One
Differing perceptions of sport and politics in East and West

No pattern of sport can be properly understood without reference to a country's physical and social environment. Sport in the USA or the UK, just as in the USSR or Cuba, cannot be divorced from the nation's climate and historical traditions, the political and economic order, military and international considerations, and much besides. Moreover, a nation's pattern of sport is by no means monolithic, natural, or static. It consists of multifarious ingredients of a regional, class, gender, religious, age and ethnic nature; and it is in constant flux.

The specific form 'sport' takes in any culture is peculiar to that particular culture or social group at a specific time. There is no such entity as capitalist sport or communist sport, however similar may be many of the structural features. It would therefore be as mistaken to posit the British/US or Soviet/Chinese models as representative of capitalist and communist development as it would to export them unadapted. Both have been tried.

There are, none the less, certain common features of the dominant sports system in some economically advanced Western countries, on the one hand, and certain common characteristics in some economically advanced communist nations, on the other. In part this is due to the seminal role played by Britain and the USSR in their respective historical 'spheres of influence'. But if we are looking for the distinctiveness of a sports system solely or mainly in ideology (capitalist or communist), we will be barking up the wrong tree. We shall be missing the unique, historically conditioned cultural heritage of each society.

Historically, Western attitudes to sport have been strongly influenced by the evolution of an organised sports movement in the latter part of the nineteenth century, in step with urban-industrial growth. Individual enthusiasts from among the leisured classes pioneered the development of certain organised sports, gave them their rules and conventions, vocabulary and ethics, equipment and dress. Much of this came from

9

Great Britain (even today show-jumpers don the attire of the English country squire). The reasons for this seminal role have to be sought in the fact that, as the major scene of the Industrial Revolution, Britain had by the mid-nineteenth century accumulated considerable surplus wealth, efficient communications at home and abroad, and a prosperous leisure class eager to pioneer sports for its own disportment in the new urban environment.

This new ruling class did not invent a new sports system, it usurped the people's games and the casual field sports of the gentry, transformed the entire mode of games playing and, initially, made the sports exclusive to its own social, sexual and racial groups – chiefly by means of the amateur code which it created. Owing to the evolving nature of society, these 'new' sports tended to be those that could be played in town parks and gardens, on the roads and in halls. In addition, the colonial emissaries took their sports with them all over the world, so implanting their model among native elites who adapted it to their own needs and conditions.

There also grew up a virtual obsession in Victorian thinking with relationships between moral and physical virtues in the context of the great upheavals of the industrial, social and political revolutions. Sports were developed, especially at British 'public' (i.e. private) schools, as a means of character formation, of training future captains of industry and empire in such character traits as loyalty, self-discipline, competitiveness and leadership ensconced in an unwritten code of sporting ethics. Some of the new sports missionaries, or 'muscular Christians' as some of them were known, whose social conscience balked at the social exclusivity of the new sports, tried to spread the sports and their 'noble' values amongst the lower orders, not so much as leisure pursuits but more as vehicles for training body and mind.

The international embodiment of the Victorian world-view of sport was the Olympic movement, whose original exclusivity in class, gender and racial terms, inscribed in its amateur code, effectively confined competition to male scions of the gentry and bourgeoisie in the imperial nations. The Olympic movement, for its part, adopted the nation-state as the central unit of modern social morphology and accepted athletes into the Games (the first being held in Athens in 1896) only as formal 'representatives' of nations. In complementarity, however, its own ideology, 'Olympism', lay great emphasis on transcending national and cultural boundaries and rivalries in the name of a common humanity through co-operative effort in sport.

There are a number of long-lasting facets of this philosophy of sport that highlight its distinction from the sports philosophy as articulated by many developing nations, and especially the communist states. Without an understanding of these facets (for, being born with them, we often take them as 'natural' and 'universal') we will not be able to appreciate the different philosophy of the communist world.

First in the Victorian world-view, sport was regarded as the concern only of the individual, a part of life unconnected with classes and social values, with economics and politics. It was confined to the 'garden of human activities', and often to a *private* garden at that. Scant attention was paid to sport as a political or social phenomenon. Vestiges of this attitude still remain in some Western countries: in the hostility to state involvement in sport, in the proliferation of independent sports bodies and clubs, in the divorcing of school and college sport and physical education from 'academic studies', in the relatively low status of sports studies in higher education.

As we shall see in the next chapter, dominant communist philosophy not only implicitly accepts the interwining of sport and politics, but stresses the primacy of sport in affecting politics and the potential of sport as a medium of social change.

A second inherited Victorian tradition is the perception of sport as being centred on bodily performance, with the body preferentially understood in European metaphysics as a 'natural' (i.e. universal and in itself unmediated) fact subject to discoverable laws. The acceptance of a dualist metaphysic in the nineteenth century led to a sharp separation of mind from body, a concern with things of the mind at the expense of bodily activities. Under the strong influence of Christian theology, this distinction of mind and body was sometimes exaggerated into an antagonism, so that body and soul were seen as warring parties, with the body cast as the villain of the piece.

The legacy of such attitudes long resulted in official denigration of professional sport and qualified administrators and coaches, in sport being regarded as unworthy of a profession. The low status of physical by contrast with cerebral and aesthetic activities is still apparent in Western countries through the relatively weak provision of opportunities for developing giftedness. While music and ballet residential schools are readily accepted, sports boarding schools are not. While early training for gifted and (ungifted) pianists and ballet dancers is accepted, such training for promising athletes is generally not. To many in the West, mental and physical activities are still considered

11

separately, with overwhelming priority accorded to the cerebral and aesthetic.

A similar division persists in regard to science and medicine, on the one hand, and sport on the other. In most Western cultures, science and sport are seen as disjunctive categories. True, natural science and medicine contribute to sporting practice in such forms as biomechanics, diet and sports injury clinics; and scientific practice is frequently discussed – as are politics and economics – in sporting language, metaphors and analogies. But the two domains are rarely considered to possess any deeper relationship. Science, after all, is the zenith of 'cerebral' activity, sport of 'corporeal'. This is yet another example of the pervasive ontological and religious dualism that separates 'mind' or 'soul' from 'body' or 'matter'.

The parochial and historically conditioned nature of this outlook has to be comprehended in order to understand not only the communist world-view of physical and mental culture as being essential for the all-round development of the individual personality and, ultimately, for the health of society, but also the traditional (Confucian) notion of physical activities being imbued primarily with spiritual content (mind over matter).

Clearly, a great deal has changed since the time when organised sports were being defined in the West. International sport is no longer a European and North American monopoly, but a socio-cultural system that reaches to a varying extent the national lives of over 160 countries (the number that had representatives at the 1988 Summer Olympics in South Korea) in all regions of the globe. The sports movement is no longer the fiefdom of a handful of aristocratic or would-be artistocratic pedagogues, athletes and humanist reformers, but a univeral army of officials, coaches, athletes, medics, entrepreneurs, travel agents, security officials, politicians, journalists and academics. Although West European and North American elites and ideological values still dominate the actions of this world army, far-reaching and profound changes are under way. For a start, West Europeans and North Americans may still prevail in the bureaucracy and decision making of the Olympic Games and sports federations, but they no longer dominate the performance. In summer and winter Olympics, and in many individual world championships, it is athletes from non-Western states that today take the major prizes.

Not only that. The world now has alternative patterns of sport or, rather, multiple paths of sports/recreation/games development to emulate. Developing countries no longer have to join the 'civilised' world community on Western terms through Western sports. They can write their own history, develop or resurrect their own folk traditions, or even adapt the pattern of physical culture pioneered by the Bolsheviks in Soviet Russia, or the Maoists in China, or the Castroists in Cuba. The states of Eastern Europe now have the opportunity to plough a middle furrow between East and West. The choice today is incomparably greater than it was just a short time ago.

The West too is faced with a choice and a dilemma. It is in awkward transition from the period in which its military, technological and economic resources ensured both imperialist domination and the self-delusion that 'world history' was but a mere extension of Western history. In denying to other regions of the world any history beyond the shadows of its own, the West lost any real sense of its own place in the world system it had done so much to create. Although Western mass media, educational curricula and politics remain parochial and hegemonic in many ways, a new awareness of the varieties of 'otherness' in the world is slowly percolating through, not least from other, including communist, sports systems.

Western sport in the main is in transition from the amateur-elitist dominant ethos and institutions to the commercial–professional ethos and institutions. The clash between the two has occurred in different forms in various countries. At best the evolution towards the new ethos has produced encouragement for the spotting, nurturing and rewarding of sports talent, the development of sports schools and the entry into sport of a far wider social community than ever before. At worst, it has resulted in sport that is looked upon as a source of profit, for commercial agents and go-betweens, for hand-outs and retainers, for governments that shift their responsibility for sport on to willing entrepreneurs whose interest is not sport but its exploitation in order to sell their product and line their pockets.

But these are not the only social forces at work in sport. Within Western societies, liberation movements and demands for increased resources by ethnic, religious and disadvantaged social groups, including women, are radically altering the overall picture of sport. Here again the alternative experience of non-Western communities has helped to open up the options, revealed the development of dominant sport in the West as being restricted to a particular time and class. Sport is clearly no longer perceived as being universal in nature, form, or meaning.

As far as communist nations are concerned, it does not help our understanding of the world, let alone sport, to look at them as a coherent 'bloc'. At least until the late 1980s, the communist states conventionally comprised the nine states of Eastern Europe, seven in Asia (Afghanistan, China, Kampuchea, Laos, Mongolia, North Korea and Vietnam) and the Caribbean state of Cuba. In a broader sense, if we include states with Marxist governments, we have to add ten African nations, the South American countries of Surinam and Guyana (and, until recently, of Nicaragua), as well as the People's Democratic Republic of Yemen in the Middle East.

The list is ever changing: in the first three-quarters of the twentieth century it expanded fairly rapidly, but the last quarter is already seeing a contraction, with the desertion from the communist 'camp' of several East European countries. None the less, the communist states still constitute a sizeable chunk of the world's land mass and population. The USSR alone occupies a sixth of the earth's land surface, and China possesses a quarter of the world's people. Together the communist nations account for about a third of humanity and of terra firma.

While some communist states are large (USSR and China), some are middling (Vietnam (60m), most are smallish (about 15m) and a few are tiny (Laos, Albania, Mongolia). Some are relatively economically advanced, some are very poor; most are developing states which are economically and socially (in terms of vital statistics) well behind the West's economically advanced countries. With minor exceptions, the communist nations are societies whose recent or present development rests on an overwhelmingly illiterate peasant population bearing the standard features of social backwardness (in average life expectancy, infantile mortality, morbidity, rural–urban balance, GNP). Most of them started their 'industrial revolution' up to 200 years after the advanced Western states.

What many of them have in common is that they are modernising societies which belong to the great bulk of the world's people and over three-quarters of the globe's nations: they are relatively poor, agricultural, young (in post-colonial or post-revolutionary development) and mainly socialist in respect of central planning, dominant political ideology, and their predominant public ownership (though not necessarily popular control) of the means of production.

A further factor of relevance to our understanding is the nature of their birth (and even demise) as socialist states and of their current perceptions of socialism. Some won socialism through popular revolution:

the USSR in 1917, Yugoslavia and Albania in 1945–46, China in 1949, Cuba in 1959 and Vietnam (as a unified state) in 1975–76; some had a semi-democratic transition to socialism (Czechoslovakia in 1948, North Korea in 1949, Laos and Kampuchea in 1975); others had socialism thrust upon them by the presence of the Soviet Army (most of Eastern Europe after the Second World War, and Afghanistan after 1978) – just as France, Greece and Italy had pro-Western governments thrust upon them in the wake of the Second World War, and some South American countries today have US-imposed regimes with no democratic support. Poland, Romania, Tibet and Afghanistan have had their equivalents in Panama, Chile, El Salvador and Guatemala. The world is not always what its peoples would have it be, given the choice.

When we use terms like 'the communist nations', we have to be aware that often they conceal a multitude of differences. In any case, with some the term 'communist' is fast becoming an anachronism. Far better is it to do each state the justice of seeing it as a separate nation with its own traditions and history, culture and geography, its own personality, as unique and different as are the nations of the West – as Greece from the United Kingdom, the USA from France, Ireland from Canada, Italy from Germany. Sport is but a reflection of that uniqueness.

Chapter Two
Communist sport: the philosophical roots

Future education . . . will, in the case of every child over a certain age, combine productive work with instruction and gymnastics, both as a means of improving work efficiency and as the only way to produce fully-developed human beings.[1]

A problem in trying to identify the penumbra of meaning surrounding the concept of 'communist sport' is that nuances change in usage – in the various communist cultures, among different social groups and, at times, within a single culture. This varying interpretation of 'sport' is, of course, not confined to communist states; 'sport' does not conjure up the same images to the British, French, North Americans, or Japanese. With some nations even lack of the word 'sport' deprives us of a common tongue: hence 'athletics' for North Americans, 'idrett' for Scandinavians, 'physical culture' for Russians and other East Europeans, and 't'i yu' for Chinese. In divided Germany, West used 'Sport', East used 'Körperkultur' (physical culture). Each term and concept bears its own range of interpretations.

The very meaning of 'sport' – the games various societies have created, their mode of playing, the rules and conventions that govern them, the importance attached to them by athletes, promoters and spectators – has always been inextricably bound up with the nature of that society. This is apparent in the 'games' of Ancient Greece and Rome (from the propitiary festivals on Mount Olympus to the military training of Sparta and Crete, from the commercial 'circuses' of Rome to the physical culture of Athens); the jousts and tournaments of Renaissance Italy, the European gymnastics system (of Guts Muts, Jahn, Ling and Lesgaft) so closely linked to national regeneration following the Napoleonic Wars; the competitive 'modern' sports pioneered for urban–industrial capitalist society mainly at the British public schools, and the commercial 'spectaculars' of the contemporary world. Such sporting activities cannot be understood apart from the nexus of social relations which characterise social life at different historical moments. But the relationship is not a simple one. The dominant pattern of sport in Britain or the USSR today, for example, has not evolved in any orderly or rational way so much as it has developed as a result of numerous and complex struggles between different groups in the history of the two nations.

We should therefore proceed with caution in defining 'communist sport'. Let us start by examining its philosophical roots.

Marx, Engels and Lenin

Much is made in communist literature on sport of the debt owed to Marx, Engels and Lenin. Since all three wrote virtually nothing directly on the subject, this may sound a strange debt; it is, however, the implications of their philosophy that are generally referred to.

To be sure, Marx was not the originator of the communist idea. The concept of a communal life, in which sharing and community ownership were valued over individualism and the acquisition of private property, has been expressed down the ages. The Greek *polis* inspired Plato to write about his ideal society in the *Republic*, which is one of the earliest examples of Western literature that advocated the sharing of possessions. In the course of Western history, numerous eminent works have advocated a communist society. Among the better known are Sir Thomas More's *Utopia* (1516), Tommaso Campanella's *City of the Sun* (1623), Jonathan Swift's *Gulliver's Travels* (1726), Samuel Butler's *Erewhon* (1872) and William Morris's *A Dream of John Ball* (1874).

The social and economic frustrations of early industrial capitalism caused a host of writers in the nineteenth century to express their views on communism: Robert Owen and William Morris in Britain, Saint-Simon and Fourier in France, to name but a few. They outlined a magnificent vision of a different, alternative, non-competitive, co-operative, or socialist society (with its own pattern of sport based on the principles of co-operation and solidarity). But their vision of socialism, inspiring though it was, tended to be *utopian*. They thought that socialism could come at any time, that the evils and waste of capitalism had only to be explained, a workable alternative to it only to be worked out and made known, for everybody to agree to ending it. In short, like Charles Dickens in his novels, they imagined they could persuade the rich and powerful, the landlords and capitalists, to renounce their wealth and power and to assist in organising the new society. For these reasons, such early socialist ideas remained visionary and utopian.

When Marx and Engels came to express their ideas, therefore, they had a long tradition behind them. But they did not intend simply to add their names to the list of those endorsing communistic ideas; rather, they wished to be distinguished from them. Whereas others had seen their utopian hopes fade with the passage of time, Marx and Engels were convinced that their 'scientific' approach would ensure success.

Karl Marx (1818–83), with his friend and collaborator Friedrich Engels (1820–95), explained how and why society developed from the first tribal society ('primitive communism') to class society (slave-owning society, then feudal society and then capitalism) and how it would develop onwards through socialism to a classless communist society. Together they analysed capitalist society, how it arose, what were the contradictions and class struggles within it, how it was at first progressive compared to feudalism but then became reactionary, a brake on social progress. Their analysis was based mainly on a study of modern industrial capitalism in the country of its birth and where it had reached its pinnacle of development when they were writing – namely, Britain. They showed how the working people were exploited under capitalism and how capitalism led to economic crises.

They indicated that the possibility of socialism arose at a given stage of capitalist development, and that it could only be achieved under the leadership and through the struggle of the working class and its allies. They explained that the state was not something eternal, but that it arose with class society and served as an instrument of power of the ruling class. Socialism, they said, could not be achieved within the framework of capitalism and the capitalist state. The common people would have to take political power into their own hands, put an end to the old capitalist state and replace it with a state that would serve them, the majority, and not the capitalists. The rule of capital would be replaced by the rule of the working class and its allies (a situation which Marx called the 'dictatorship of [that is, by] the proletariat') and the working people would use power to defend their new society from reaction at home and abroad and, step by step, to build socialism. If Marx and Engels were the ideologues and theorists of modern communism, Vladimir Ilych Lenin (1870–1924) may be called its strategist and tactician. Lenin developed the thought of Marx and Engels in the changing world at the turn of the century, particularly in Russia. He showed how capitalism developed into monopoly capitalism and imperialism, and he outlined the effect of imperialism both on the colonial peoples and on the workers within the imperialist countries themselves. While Marx and Engels spoke philosophically of spontaneous revolution, Lenin set to to bring it about. In order to head off the drift to reformism, revisionism and economism, he organised a tightly knit, highly disciplined party, the Bolshevik or Communist Party (the most effective type of revolutionary organisation in the oppressive conditions of tsarist Russia). Lenin, then, was concerned with practical details, and he contributed the following concepts to modern communist thought: the importance of a highly disciplined, united communist party; the need for a professional, dedicated band of revolutionaries to lead the party and be in charge of implementing the revolution; and the importance of obtaining the support of the underdeveloped, colonial areas of the world in the struggle against capitalism and imperialism. He thus proposed new revolutionary possibilities by extending the vision from the advanced industrial centres to the colonial and semi-colonial (like tsarist Russia) countries.

The work of Marx, Engels and Lenin is subject to much debate and analysis among communists today. A number of different 'schools of Marxism' have grown up, and each has a particular interpretation of what is and what is not important in their writing. This often extends to promoting some documents to the exclusion of others. Since Russia was the first country successfully to carry through a communist revolution and attempt to build a socialist society, its leaders, particularly Stalin, who dominated the country from Lenin's death in 1924 to his own death in 1953, have had enormous influence on the rest of the world in their interpretations of 'Marxism–Leninism' based on their own policies and Soviet conditions. As a consequence, much of what are today regarded as univeral Marxist–Leninist axioms are no more than expedient dogma particular to Soviet development and Stalin's policies.

Marx, Engels and Lenin had in fact insisted that their philosophy was by no means a static dogma, but an approach to understanding the world, a guide to action. With the far-reaching changes that have occurred all over the world this century, it is perhaps inevitable that the body of thought and practice associated with the founding fathers should be developed, modified and even interpreted in different ways.

Marxism–Leninism and sport

Marx and Engels

At the time Marx and Engels were writing, in the mid nineteenth century, metaphysics was, as indicated above, in the grip of a dualism that separated mind from matter. Marx and Engels rejected the dualist philosophy and emphasised that not only was there an intimate relationship existing between matter and mind, but that the former largely determined the latter. In their view, political and social institutions and the ideas, images and ideologies through which people understand the world in which they live, their place within it and themselves – all these ultimately derived from the 'economic base' of society, the class relations into which people had to enter with one another in order to produce. As Marx put it,

> In the social production which people carry on they enter into certain relationships which are indispensable and independent of their wills; these relations of production correspond to a certain stage of development of their material powers of production. The sum total of these relations of production constitutes the economic structure of society – the real foundation on which rise legal and political superstructures and to which correspond certain forms of social consciousness. The mode of production in material life determines the general character of the social, political and spiritual processes of life. It is people's social existence that determines their consciousness, not the consciousness that determines social existence.[2]

This fundamental Marxist tenet contains certain implications for recreation.

(a) Since the human psychosomatic organism develops and changes under the impact of external conditions, including the social environment, subjection to physical exercise not only develops that part of the body to which it is directed, but it also has an effect on the body as a whole – on the personality. A strong bond exists between social and individual development and between an individual's physical and mental development. Societies are likely to seek to shape this development.

(b) In liberal capitalist society, whose prevailing ideology is that of 'independent' decision-making and 'free' contracting between 'equal' social atoms, sport has normally been regarded as the concern only of the individual, a feature of life unconnected with classes and social values, with economics and society's mode of production; little attention has been paid to it as a social phenomenon. To the Marxist, however, sport is part of the social superstructure and therefore affected by the prevailing relations of production – not something 'in itself' and so divorced from politics; a society's pattern of sport will ultimately depend on the specifics of the society's socio-economic formation, its class relationships. Moreover, says Marx, 'with a change in the economic foundation, the entire immense superstructure is more or less rapidly transformed'.[3] The nature of sport can therefore be expected by the Marxist to alter with any change to a new socio-economic formation.

(c) The acceptance of a dualist metaphysic, a sharp separation of body and mind, had often led to a concern with things of the mind at the expense of bodily activities. Marx emphasised that practical activities have a decisive impact on all human development in the broadest sense. None more so than work, through which people can change themselves as well as nature:

Work is, in the first place, a process in which both people and nature participate, and in which people of their own accord start, regulate and control the material reactions between themselves and nature. They oppose themselves to nature as one of her own forces, setting in motion arms and legs, head and hands, the natural forces of the body, in order to appropriate nature's productions in a form adapted to human wants. By thus acting on the external world and changing it, they at the same time change their own nature.[4]

This proposition implies a strong link between work and such other bodily activities as physical exercise and games-playing. It has led some Marxist historians to seek the origin of games and sports in practices in primitive society, leading to the improvement of physical dexterity and utilitarian skills vital to working and hunting. In this they refer to Engels: 'The use of various forms of weapons in work and military activity among primitive peoples developed their mental and physical abilities.'[5]

From his studies of early bourgeois society, Marx came to the conclusion that production was actually inhibited by, *inter alia*, the denial to the workers of time for recreation which would help restore their energy for production and make it more efficient. Marx was concerned with civil society's needs for workers to obtain more free time – not only for pure leisure but also for recuperating their strength and applying themselves more vigorously to productive work after reasonable rest and recreation. What he saw as the sheer wasteful inefficiency of the capitalist production of his day in neglecting the recreative functions of play agitated him: 'The capitalist mode of production [because it absorbs surplus labour] produces . . . not only the deterioration of human labour-power by robbing it of its normal, moral and physical, conditions of development and function. It produces also the premature exhaustion and death of this labour-power itself.'[6] Elsewhere, he writes that 'from the point of view of the direct process of production, this saving [of working time] may be considered as the production of *basic capital*; man himself is that basic capital.'[7] Physically fit and mentally alert workers are better able to cope with new industrial skills and increasingly complex technology and to have higher productivity by showing less absenteeism and greater activity on the job.

Modern industry, however, objectively requires more than physically fit workers; it needs versatile, fully developed individuals, healthy in body and in mind. In the education system of the future, therefore, citizens were to be given, Marx advised, the opportunity for balanced all-round education, in which physical education was to be an integral part; the system would consist of three elements combining training of the mind with training of the body:

First, mental education.
Second, bodily education, such as is given in schools of gymnastics, and by military exercises.
Third, technical training, which acquaints the pupil with the basic principles of all processes of production and, simultaneously, gives him the habits of handling elementary instruments of all trades.[8]

In the English Factory Acts Marx had seen the germs of the prototypes of such a system in which mental and physical education would be combined with manual labour to improve social production and to produce all-round individuals: 'From the Factory system budded, as Robert Owen has shown in detail, the germ of the education of the future, an education that will, in the case of every child over a given age, combine productive work with instruction and gymnastics, both as a means of improving work efficiency and as the only way to produce fully-developed human beings.'[9]

Whether games-playing contained its own justification within itself or whether its value was to be sought in ulterior ends was not a question specifically raised by Marx. The Marxist vision of the future, however, does seem to imply that work and physical recreation will merge, or that work will be elevated to the plane of recreation by the removal of the yokes of specialisation and compulsion. But Marx evidently did not envisage recreation under communism as simply games, but rather as a fusion of work-like activities with play. In this, he affirmed a principal criterion of playful activities, namely, that they are freely chosen and are pursued for their inherent pleasure rather than for practical results.

To sum up, Marx provided few clear-cut guidelines on physical culture. On the one hand, he stressed the interdependence of work and physical recreation and, on the other, he saw the playful use of energy as contributing to the enrichment of the personality, or self-realisation. But, as has been pointed out, 'There is no *one* Marx. The various presentations of his work which we can construct from his books, pamphlets, articles, letters, written at different times in his own development, depend upon our point of interest, and we may not take any one of them to be The Real Marx.'[10] The same might be said of Lenin. That is not to say there is no consistency in the writings of Marx or Lenin, no *Marxism* or *Leninism*.

Leninism

If Marx made scant direct reference to sport, Lenin was scarcely more prolific on the subject – despite the sixty volumes of his writings in the latest Soviet edition. Unlike Marx, who personally abhorred any physical exercises,[11] Lenin was, moreover, an active practitioner of physical fitness and sport in his own life. As a British observer has put it 'Of all the prominent Russian revolutionaries, he was the keenest sportsman. From boyhood he had been fond of shooting and skating. Always a great walker, he became a keen mountaineer, a lively cyclist, and an impatient fisherman.'[12] Particularly during his periods of imprisonment and exile, he valued fitness as a stimulant to mental alertness. While in a St Petersburg prison, he wrote that he did 'gymnastics with great pleasure and value *every day*' (emphasis in original).[13] In a letter from Munich to his sister, then in prison in Russia, he urged her 'to do gymnastics and have a good rub-down every day. It is absolutely essential when you are alone . . . force yourself to do several dozen exercises (without stopping). That is very important.'[14] Of his personal preferences, his wife recalled that he enjoyed ice-skating, shooting, hiking, the Russian folk game of *gorodki* and cycling – even to the extent of ordering bicycles for his wife and himself from Berlin through the Russian Sports Society *Nadezhda* (Hope) in 1910.[15] His favourite pastime – like that of several other *émigré* Russian intellectuals – was chess, which he played regularly (many games by correspondence with Lunacharsky, later to become the first Commissar of Enlightenment, as the education minister was named, and with the writer Maxim Gorky). On his return to Russia in 1917 after an exile of twelve years, however, his wife reports that 'Vladimir Ilyich had to give up chess, his favourite game, because it involved too much of his time'.[16] He did, none the less, become honorary president of the Moscow Chess Society in November 1922.

Lenin's sporting activity may seem to have little relevance to an understanding of sport in communist states. One must bear in mind, however, the influence Lenin has had on all communist societies, as well as the Soviet establishment's cult of Lenin and penchant for looking to Lenin's personal example when seeking to justify current policies. Official advocacy of daily exercise and such pursuits as chess have thus been able to call on Lenin's own preferences. The desire to promote certain forms of recreation has certainly resulted in the highlighting of individual aspects of Lenin's habits and mode of life.

What are clearly more important are his writings on the subject of sport and physical education. Like Marx's, Lenin's educational philosophy favoured a combination of the training of the mind and the body: 'It is impossible to visualise the ideal of a future society without a combination of instruction and productive labour, nor can productive labour without parallel instruction and physical education be put on a plane required by the modern level of technology and the state of scientific knowledge.'[17] In his article 'Karl Marx', he refers to Marx's appraisal of Robert Owen's school in Lanarkshire – which combined mental and physical education with manual work – as the germ of the education of the future.[18] This model even found some reflection in the decree 'On Compulsory Instruction in the Military Art', passed in the crisis months of 1918, which brought into being the military-sports organisation Vsevobuch (which took charge of all sports organisation between 1917 and 1921). Its chairman, Nikolai Podvoisky, later described the decree as 'combining gymnastics and all forms of physical development and training with general and military training in our country. By this decree, physical culture was introduced into the working people's common education system, their training for defending their country and for highly-productive and varied work.'[19] He went on to stress Lenin's contribution to the decree: 'Vladimir Ilyich often stressed, and the decree established, the correct view of popular physical education as a means of obtaining the harmonious all-round development of the individual.'[20]

Lenin, therefore, derived from and shared with Marx the notion of potential fully-developed individuals, of men and women who could not attain the full measure of their latent abilities under capitalism. 'We must develop people's capabilities, uncover their talents which are an untapped source in people and which capitalism has repressed, crushed and stifled in their thousands of millions.'[21] Under socialism and complete communism, however, everyone would have a chance to choose the physical activity they wanted to pursue and to attain complete self-realisation. It would 'not merely satisfy the needs of its members, but ensure *complete* welfare and free *all-round* development of *all* members of society' (emphasis in original).[22]

Influenced by his own experience of physical and mental training during periods of privation and confronted by the practical problems of power, Lenin added an emphasis on character training that was absent in Marx. He recognised the effects that sport might have, for instance, upon the development of qualities of character valuable to individuals and society, upon the social behaviour of citizens and upon the promotion of health. In his comments on the advocates of 'free love' and on the hard left in the cultural revolution, Lenin took a position on the moral effects of sport which was not far removed from that of English 'muscular Christians' like Dr Arnold of Rugby and the novelists Thomas Hughes and Charles Kingsley: 'Young people especially need to have a zest for living and be in good spirits. Healthy sport – gymnastics, swimming, hiking, all manner of physical exercise – should be combined as much as possible with a variety of intellectual interests, study, analysis and investigation . . . That will give young people more than extraneous theories and discussions about sex . . . Healthy bodies, healthy minds!'[23] Sport would also safeguard clean-limbed youngsters from such vices as drunkenness and smoking – as the decree 'On Curbing Tobacco-Smoking' was intended to do in 1919. When asked how young people should spend their spare time, Lenin once replied, 'Young men and women of the Soviet land should live life beautifully and to the full both in public and private. Wrestling, work, study, sport, making merry, singing, dreaming – these are things young people should make the most of.'[24] Games-playing, then, was, in Lenin's view, conducive to moral as well as physical health; it was a valuable ingredient in character training. One can imagine Lenin's ideal young people (not unlike the heroes of Kingsley's *Westward Ho* and Hughes's *Tom Brown's Schooldays*) drawn in glowing colours, adorned with every sort of athletic accomplishment and displaying the excellence of simple understanding and the urge to serve the proletarian cause. The resolution passed by the Third All-Russia Congress of the Russian Young Communist League (October 1920) – at which Lenin spoke – surely reflected his views on sport: 'The physical culture of the younger generation is an essential element in the overall system of communist upbringing of young people, aimed at creating harmoniously developed human beings, creative citizens of communist society. Today, physical culture also has direct practical aims: (1) preparing young people for work; and (2) preparing them for military defence of Soviet power.'[25]

This, the first clear-cut official statement on the aims of Soviet sport, makes no bones about the rational use of physical education for purposes of work and defence. It does, however, hint that, once society is on its feet and socialism moving towards communism, utilitarian–instrumental aims will give way to self-realisation. None the less, here (some years before Soviet industrialisation commenced, but in the midst of çivil war) was a commitment to use sport for labour and military purposes.

On another occasion, Lenin indicated the powerful social force that sport might be in contributing to women's emancipation. 'It is our urgent task to draw working women into sport . . . If we can achieve that and get them to make full use of the sun, water and fresh air for fortifying themselves, we shall bring an entire revolution in the Russian way of life.'[26] Furthermore, Podvoisky writes that Lenin stressed to him the 'huge significance of the task of Vsevobuch: correctly to train people in physical culture and so to attain through them a cultured, comradely mutual relationship between young men and women'.[27] Lenin evidently saw in sport a convenient vehicle for drawing women into public activity and an era where they could relatively quickly achieve a measure of equality with men – and be seen to do so.

Lenin, therefore, implied that there was more to sport than mere physical enjoyment; it could, and indeed should, contribute to forming the all-round individual of communist society, to character formation, especially among young people, to women's emancipation and to some – not very explicit – labour and military goals. The stress that communist leaders later put on the interdependence of sport and work, rather than on the enrichment of the personality, may well not have been where Lenin would have put it himself had he not had a war on his hands. It is evidently necessary to distinguish the immediately pre-revolutionary Lenin, say, of *State and Revolution* (the work in which he most emphasises free personal development[28]), from the Lenin in power concerned about defence and productivity. Similarly, one must distinguish the rather vague forecasts about the future ideal society made by Marx and Engels, Lenin and Trotsky in regard to the second stage of communist society or 'full communism' from their more practical remarks about its first or socialist stage. In later Soviet 'interpretations' of Lenin, made during the rapid industrialisation period, the emphasis shifts to what Podvoisky, writing in 1940 on Lenin's views on physical education, calls 'a scientific approach to military and labour methods' by means of sport and physical education, 'making them accessible to the working people so as to attain higher labour productivity'.[29]

To sum up, a Marxist–Leninist interpretation of culture, both mental and physical, including a belief in the interdependence of the mental and physical states of human beings, provides the general framework within which physical and mental recreation is viewed in all communist states. It should, however, be noted that aphorisms drawn from and myths about Lenin (or Marx, Mao, Castro, Tito, etc.) in regard to physical culture have been taken up to justify policies at particular stages of development and need not necessarily be taken as creative Marxist thinking (indeed, they have sometimes replaced it). As Marx and Lenin would readily have admitted, it is the socio-economic processes that largely fashion patterns of sport, not the prescriptions of philosophers who, to paraphrase Marx, only interpret the world.

Influence of Russia and the Soviet Union

As the pioneer of socialist revolution and construction, Soviet Russia (the Soviet Union from 1922) inevitably laid its imprint on other countries undergoing such processes later. All the nations of Eastern Europe, and many outside – such as China and Cuba – have been strongly affected in their sports development by the pattern established in the Soviet Union. All therefore share similar functional and utilitarian aims for sport, the state control and structure (and financing), the singular involvement in sport of military and paramilitary organisations. In regard to China, for example, 'To a great extent the Soviet model of physical culture has been adapted by the Chinese who have translated Soviet physical culture manuals, their scientific data and approach, their *GTO* [national fitness programme] system and their pedagogical techniques.'[30]

Similarly, following the establishment of the German Democratic Republic (GDR) in 1949, a GDR sports delegation visited the USSR with the express purpose of studying Soviet experience and transplanting Soviet methods and institutions into the GDR. Attention was focused on the physical education programme within the education system, professional training, the sports rankings pyramid, and sports medicine. So the Soviet fitness programme and sports administrative structure were directly transferred to the GDR, Soviet textbooks were translated, and Soviet specialists 'imported' – all this despite the long German sports experience which, in many ways, was far superior to that in the Soviet Union.

The same process occurred in other parts of Eastern Europe, sometimes in quite slavish imitation of the USSR, even though Soviet sports institutions had developed largely from pre-revolutionary and Stalinist Russia to meet specifically Russian and Soviet requirements and policies.

The October 1917 Revolution in Russia certainly brought a rupture with the past in many ways; yet several aspects of Soviet sport, as of other areas of social life (education, for example), still show, if not continuity with the past, at least strong influence by factors having their origins outside the Soviet period. It would be wrong to imagine that a totally new structure, inspired only by new ideas, was erected after 1917. The roots of Soviet sport in part lie deep in Russian history, in the Russian people's habits and traditions, the Russian climate, the Russian state's preoccupation with external and internal enemies, the intellectual ferment of Russian society in the late nineteenth and early twentieth centuries.

It would have been strange had these currents played much less a role in shaping the practice of sport in the Soviet Union and other communist countries than the social thought of foreign philosophers – and these, it must be realised, included Locke and especially, Rousseau, as well as Marx and Engels. In addition, foreign practice, in the form of the pattern of organised sport pioneered for industrial society by Britain, of the gymnastics schools and movements of Germany, the Scandinavian countries and what is now Czechoslovakia (the Sokol movement), and Prussian military training all put their imprint on Soviet sport and physical education. Moreover, individual foreigners were influential both in the practice and in the organisation of specific sports in Russia (particularly in boxing, soccer and fencing). Not always has their contribution been recognised. For example, the Soviet fitness programme, inaugurated in 1931 and initially called 'Be Prepared for Work and Defence' was, as its title suggests, based on the targets set by Baden-Powell in his Scout movement for 'marksman' and 'athlete' badges.[31]

In the official Soviet view, sport is considered to be part of physical culture, which has four components:[32]

 (i) organised physical education;
 (ii) playful activities or games;
(iii) all forms of (socially approved) active leisure pursuits; and
(iv) organised sport.

Organised physical education consists of general physical exercises with a therapeutic motive uppermost – for example, morning exercises or PE in school; physical exercises with a sporting bias, such as gymnastics and acrobatics; physical exercises for utilitarian work purposes (known as 'production gymnastics' – exercises during work breaks at workplaces); and physical exercise for mass aesthetic or artistic display.

Playful activities may be individual, group, or mass games which, although not a strictly regulated obligation, are based on generally accepted rules and relatively stable conditions of conduct.

Active leisure pursuits are included in physical culture as long as they are considered to add to the mental and physical well-being of the individual or to that of the community in general. Some pursuits are at times referred to more narrowly as 'tourism', which consists of a variety of organised outdoor activities including hiking, camping, boating and rock-climbing.

Organised sport is regarded as a playful, competitive physical or mental activity, based on rules and norms, with the object of achieving a result.

In Soviet writings the word 'sport' is interpreted variously. As a leading Soviet sports theorist, Nikolai Ponomaryov, has noted, 'some writers take sport as the dominant form of expression of physical culture; they therefore use the concept "sport" as a synonym for the concept "physical culture" '.[33] Moreover, the combined expression 'physical culture and sport' (as in the USSR Committee on Physical Culture and Sport) is commonly found in Soviet writings on sport, even though in Soviet theory, sport is merely a component of physical culture and not something separate. The same concepts (and muddled thinking) have prevailed in other (former) communist states – for example, *Körperkultur* (physical culture) in the GDR. Compare the Deutsche Hochschule für Körperkultur in Leipzig with West Germany's Deutsche Sporthochschule in Cologne.

The four components in the Soviet framework together comprise physical culture, which itself is regarded as part of the overall culture of society. It is, 'The sum total of social achievements associated with people's physical development and education . . . [It is] part of the overall culture of society and represents all measures taken to make people healthy and to improve their physical abilities.'[34]

This rather broad and explicitly instrumental definition, perhaps predictable in a planned 'conscious' society, implies that sport may be a separate sector of culture, but is regarded as an integral part of a broadly

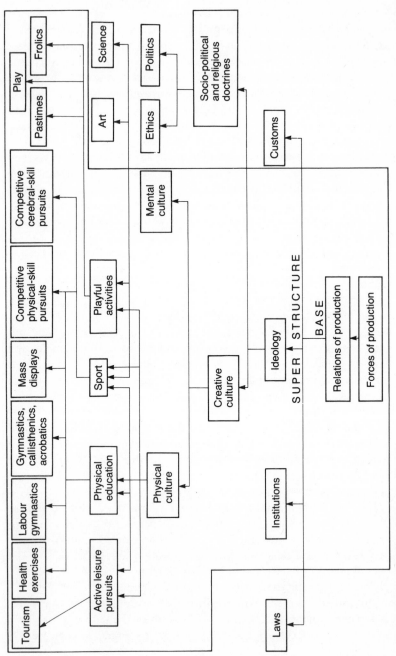

Figure 1 *Sport in society: a Soviet Marxist view*

conceived sphere of cultural life. In terms of its social significance, it is seen, to use the Marxist terms current in the USSR, as part of the cultural 'superstructure' of society resting on the 'base' of the relations of production; it is therefore expected to vary in nature and function in different types of society.

Figure 1 represents an attempt to portray the Soviet view of the component parts of physical culture and their interrelationship. Given this conceptual framework, sport is regarded as being on a par with mental culture with important functions to discharge: 'The ultimate goal of physical culture in our country is to prepare the younger generation for a long and happy life, highly productive work for the benefit of society and for the defence of their socialist homeland.[35]
Some writers are even more explicit:

> Physical culture and sport in socialist society have a number of social functions: to contribute to the formation of a harmonious personality, to socialisation and integration, to political, moral, mental and aesthetic education, to health protection, to the development of people's physical capabilities, to the accumulation and transmission of knowledge and experience in motor activity, to rational utilisation of free time, to the forging of international cultural contacts, to greater international representation [i.e. more Soviet officials on international sports bodies], to the fight for peace and friendship among peoples, etc.[36]

Here we have an explicitly functional view of sport far removed from Western perceptions.

A major problem in defining 'communist sport' or even 'Soviet sport' is that meanings are constantly changing. As we shall see in the next chapter, during the 1920s in the USSR (and to some extent in China during the 'Cultural Revolution' period), not only did the state and members of the public tend to see sport in differing ways, but so did various competing official and semi-official groups. Thus, an army group thought of sport mainly in terms of paramilitary games and exercises; the minds of members of a trade union group turned to 'production gymnastics' and newly invented 'socialist workers' games'; a strong health group thought only in terms of 'physical culture' and used the word 'sport' itself to denigrate physical competition as an evil deriving from bourgeois society; while to the Proletarian Culture group, it conjured up dreams of socialist pageants and spectacles. Of course, diverging notions in the search for the ideal, for the forms appropriate to the new society, emerged, in the years immediately following the revolution, in all fields of culture – in literature and theatre as much as in sport.

Although official views on what constituted physical culture and sport became more uniform with the onset of full-scale industrialisation at the end of the 1920s, the terms have remained loosely defined to the present day. On the whole, official conceptualising has been governed by normative considerations – that is, promotion of state-favoured activities. While countenancing chess and draughts, for example, the state has stopped short of including such activities as dominoes and card playing in the sports movement. Until recently it had drawn distinctions within a sport: for a long time men's soccer and wrestling were included in the Soviet sports movement, while women's soccer and wrestling were not; body-building and boxing were recognised as official 'sports' as long as they kept within certain officially prescribed parameters – which are not static. In China, boxing was long proscribed, but in the late 1980s was permitted and officially encouraged not only for men, but for women too. In yet other 'sports', the state appears to be less motivated by functional than by political factors, tolerating activities such as horse-racing and folk-games as a concession to popular tastes, although they involve gambling and may imply values that go against the official ethos.

For practical purposes, this book uses the term 'sport' loosely to encompass the broad interpretations of physical culture and sport in communist countries.

Notes

1 Karl Marx, *Capital*, vol. 1 (Foreign Languages Publishing House, Moscow, 1961), pp. 483–4.
2 Karl Marx, *A Contribution to the Critique of Political Economy* (Chicago, 1904), pp. 11–12.
3 *Ibid.*, p. 13.
4 Karl Marx, *Capital*, vol. 1, p. 177.
5 Friedrich Engels, *The Origin of the Family, Private Property and the State* (Foreign Languages Publishing House, Moscow, 1958), p. 28.
6 Marx, *Capital*, vol. 1, p. 265.
7 *Ibid.*, p. 332.
8 Karl Marx, 'Instructions for the delegates of the Provisional General Council. The different questions', in Marx and Engels, *Selected Works*, vol. 2 (Progress Publishers, Moscow, 1969), p. 81.
9 Marx, *Capital*, vol. 1, pp. 483–4.
10 C. Wright Mills, *The Marxists* (Penguin, London, 1962), p. 42.
11 Yvonne Knapp, *Eleanor Marx* (Lawrence & Wishart, London, 1972), vol. 1, p. 193. The only game Marx seemed to enjoy was chess (p. 26); Engels, on the other hand, was 'an enthusiastic rider to hounds, a mighty walker and a deep drinker' (*ibid.*, p. 108).

12 Robert Bruce Lockhart, *Giants Cast Long Shadows* (Putnam, London, 1960), p. 134.
13 V. I. Lenin, *Polnoye sobranie sochineni*, vol. 55 (Politizdat, Moscow, 1968), p. 72.
14 *Ibid.*, p. 73.
15 V. Bonch-Bruyevich, *Nash Ilych: vospominaniya* (Detgiz, Moscow, 1956), p. 22.
16 N. K. Krupskaya, *Vospominaniya o V. I. Lenine*, vol. 1 (Politizdat, Moscow, 1968), p. 242.
17 V. I. Lenin, *Polnoye sobranie sochineniy*, vol. 11, p. 485.
18 V. I. Lenin, *Izbrannye proizvedeniya v 3-kh tomakh*, vol. 1 (Politizdat, Moscow, 1963), p. 53.
19 N. I. Podvoisky, 'Lenin i fizicheskoye vospitanie', *Krasny sport*, 21 January 1948, no. 4 (831), pp. 3–4.
20 *Ibid.*
21 V. I. Lenin, *Polnoye sobranie sochineniy*, vol. 11, pp. 85–6.
22 *Ibid.*, vol. 6, p. 232.
23 Clara Zetkin, *Vospominaniya o Vladimire Ilyche Lenine*, Part 2 (Gospolitizdat, Moscow, 1955), p. 84.
24 Quoted in A. Bezymensky, *Vstrecha komsomoltsev s V. I. Leninom* (Politizdat, Moscow, 1956), p. 18.
25 I. D. Chudinov (ed.), *Osnovnye postanovleniya i instruktsii po voprosam fizicheskoi kultury i sporta, 1917–1957* (Politizdat, Moscow, 1959), pp. 43–44.
26 Quoted in N. I. Podovoisky, *Rabotnitsa i fizicheskaya kultura* (Molodaya Gvardia, Moscow, 1938), p. 3.
27 N. I. Podvoisky, 'Lenin i fizicheskoye vospitanie', *op. cit.*, p. 3.
28 Free personal development will take place, wrote Lenin, as the pressure of work and state coercive functions decrease: 'Socialism will shorten the working day, raise the people to a new life, create such conditions for the majority of the population as will enable everybody, without exception, to perform state functions, and this will lead to the complete withering away of every form of state in general'. See V. I. Lenin, *Selected Works*, Vol. 2 (Moscow, 1963), p. 397.
29 Podvoisky, *op. cit.*, p. 121.
30 Robert G. Glassford and Roy A. Clumpner, 'Physical culture inside the People's Republic of China', *Physical Education around the World*, Monograph 6 (University of Alberta, Edmonton, 1973), pp. 12–13.
31 See James Riordan, 'The Russian Boy Scouts', *History Today*, XXXVIII, October 1988, p. 51.
32 See A. D. Novikov and L. P. Matveyev (eds), *Teoriya fizicheskovo vospitaniya* (Fizkultura i Sport, Moscow, 1959), pp. 95–136.
33 N. I. Ponomaryov, 'K voprosu o predmete marksistkoi sotsiologii fizicheskoi kultury i sporta', *Teoriya i praktika fizicheskoi kultury*, no. 1, 1973, p. 63.
34 *Entsiklopedichesky slovar po fizicheskoi kulture i sportu*, vol. 3 (Moscow, 1963), p. 226.
35 V. V. Belorusova, *Pedagogika* (Prosveshchenie, Moscow, 1972), pp. 182–3.
36 N. I. Ponomaryov, 'Sport i obshchestvo', *Teoriya i praktika fizicheskoi kultury*, no. 6, 1973, p. 72.

Chapter Three
Communist sport: the practical roots

What is important is not the invention of a new proletarian culture, but the development of the best forms, traditions and results of existing culture from a Marxist standpoint.[1]

The notion of communist sport was born well before the Russian Revolution of October 1917. It had its practical beginnings in the labour movement of Germany in the 1890s. The idea of workers' oppositional sport combined the concept of sport with socialist fellowship, solidarity and the possibility of playing sport in a society where the structuring of sporting activities would take place in a rational rather than a rationalised manner.

Further tentative steps were taken in elaborating worker and communist sport by some groups in Soviet Russia in the 1920s; they tried to fashion a fundamentally new pattern of recreation reflecting the requirements and values of the common people and the new socialist state. This was before Soviet sport became geared to building up a strong nation-state to fit the needs of labour and defence in the early 1930s and those of international recognition and prestige after the Second World War.

Some features of these pioneering movements remain with communist sport to this day; some have been cast into oblivion; yet others may have been shelved until the objective and subjective conditions are more conducive to their implementation. A backward glance at these theoretical and practical experiments is important for an understanding not only of the evolution of communist sport, but of international labour and sports history.

Worker sport – a socialist alternative

The principal aims of worker sport differed from country to country, but all were agreed on the basic principles: that it would give working people the chance to take part in healthy recreation and to do so in a socialist atmosphere. Socialist sport was to differ from bourgeois sport by being open to all workers, women as well as men, pink as well as brown. More than that: it was to provide a socialist alternative to bourgeois competitive sport, to commercialism, chauvinism, and the obsession with stars and records. It was to replace capitalist by socialist values and thereby lay the foundations for a true working-class culture. Hence the initial emphasis was on less competitive physical activities, such as gymnastics, acrobatics, tumbling, mass artistic displays, hiking, cycling and swimming.

The founders of worker sport believed that sport could be revolutionary, that the movement was no less salient than workers' political, trade union and co-operative movements. Sport was to play a key role in the struggle against capitalist nationalism and militarism which pervaded the allegedly politically neutral bourgeois sport organisations and, through them, corrupted young workers. So the formation of separate worker sport organisations was one way of shielding youth from bourgeois values. While capitalism fostered mistrust among workers of different nations, the worker sport organisations would band together internationally to create peace and international solidarity. They would turn sport into a new international language capable of breaking down all languages barriers.

A brief history

A worker sports movement began to emerge in the 1980s with the foundation in Germany of the Worker Gymnastics Association in conscious opposition to the nationalistic German Gymnastics Society. This was followed in Germany by the Solidarity Workers Cycling Club and the Friends of Nature Rambling Association in 1896, the Workers Swimming Association in 1897, the Free Sailing Association in 1901, the Workers Track and Field Association in 1906, the Workers Chess Association in 1912 and the Free Shooting Association in 1926. Germany soon became the natural centre of the worker sports movement, with over 350,000 worker athletes in various worker clubs even before the First World War.

Elsewhere, a Workers Rambling Association was set up in Vienna in 1895; in the same year a British Workers Cycling Club was organised about the *Clarion* newspaper. In 1898 a Socialist Wheelmen's Club came into being in the USA, and workers began to establish clubs and the umbrella Socialist Sports Athletic Federation from 1907. By 1913 there were enough members for the worker sports federations of five countries – Germany, Belgium, Britain, France and Italy – to come together at Ghent on the initiative of the Belgian socialist Gaston Bridoux to set up the Socialist Physical Culture International.

By the time the various worker federations regrouped after the war, two new tendencies were emerging, both of which were to cause schism and controversy. The first was the growing movement away from non-competitive physical recreation to competitive organised sport. So when the Ghent International was reformed in 1920 at Lucerne, it was now called the International Association for Sport and Physical Culture, renamed five years later the Socialist Workers Sport International (SWSI). This change of name reflected national developments: in Germany, the Workers Gymnastics Association became the Workers Gymnastics and Sports Society (WGSS); in Austria, a Workers Soccer Association was set up, and the *New York Call*, periodical of the American Socialist Party, sponsored a baseball league. This overall shift towards team sports and competition was evidently a response to popular pressure. It may well have reflected a transfer of values from the workplace to the sphere of leisure, a reaction to the increasingly sterile nature of rationalised work. Whatever the reason, it certainly helped to boost support for the worker sport movement.

In Germany, membership of the WGSS in the late 1920s was 1.2 million across a dozen different sports; the WGSS was able to open the most modern sports club in all Germany, the Bundesschule in Leipzig (subsequently the nucleus of the German Democratic Republic's *Deutsche Hochschule für Körperkultur*). One of its affiliates, that for cycling, not only had 320,000 members – the largest cycling organisation in the world – but also ran a co-operative cycle works.

Elsewhere, the various Austrian worker sports groups combined into a single association in 1919 (VAS, later the Austrian Workers Sport and Cultural Association – WSCA), whose membership grew from 100,000 to 250,000 by 1931. Its swimming affiliate gave free swimming lessons to over 10,000 people in 1930, and to as many as 29,000 in 1931.

Membership of the Czechoslovak worker sports movement increased to over 200,000 between the wars, and in 1921, 1927 and 1934 the Czechoslovak Worker Gymanstics Association put on sports festivals in Prague in which some 35,000 took part and 100,000 attended.

In Britain, the British Workers Sports Federation showed a steady growth after its formation in 1923, and the Clarion Cycling Club produced the National Workers Sports Association (NWSA) in 1930, the same year as the Workers Wimbledon Tennis Championships were held. As evidence of its commitment to organised sports, the NWSA entered a team, the London Labour Football Club, in a local soccer league. In 1934, the NWSA played host to workers athletes from Austria, Belgium, Czechoslovakia, Palestine and Switzerland at its Dorchester Sports Festival; in turn, British workers went abroad to worker festivals, including the Moscow Spartakiad of 1928.

Even in relatively small countries like Denmark, Finland, Norway and Switzerland, membership figures were impressive: 20,000, 41,000, 65,000 and 27,000 respectively by 1930.

The second post-war tendency was the mounting division between socialists and communists over leadership and aims of the worker sports movement. A number of worker sports organisations broke away from the Lucerne Sports International (LSI – a branch of the Bureau of the Socialist International) after the formation of the International Association of Red Sports and Gymnastics Associations (better known as Red Sport International – RSI) in Moscow in 1921, as a branch of the Communist International or Comintern. Relations between the two worker sport internationals were hostile right from the start, the RSI accusing its 'reformist' rival of diverting workers from the class struggle through its policy of political neutrality in sport. True, the socialists were not trying to turn the sport movement into an active revolutionary force: instead, it was to be a strong, independent movement within capitalist society ready, after the revolution, to implement a fully developed system of physical culture. The RSI, however, wished to build a sport international that would be a political vehicle of the class struggle: it did not want merely to produce a better sport system for workers in a capitalist world. The LSI countered that the RSI only aspired to undermine and take it over; so it banned all RSI members from its activities and all contacts with the USSR (indeed, the British Labour Home Secretary J. R. Clynes refused entry visas to Soviet soccer players in 1930).

The two internationals therefore developed separately and, as with the parent political movements, spent more time and energy fighting each other rather than the common foe. By the time they came together, in 1936, it was virtually too late to save the worker sports movement from fascist repression; the German WGSS had been one of the Nazis' first targets in 1933, the Austrian WSCA was suppressed a year later, and the Czechoslovak association two years after that.

The Worker Olympics

While the worker sports movement did not take issue with much of the Coubertin idealism concerning the modern Olympic Games, it did oppose the Games themselves and counterposed them with its own Olympiads on the following grounds.[2]

First, the bourgeois Olympics encouraged competition along national lines, whereas the Workers Olympics stressed internationalism, labour solidarity and peace. While the IOC barred German and Austrian athletes from the 1920 and 1924 Games, for example, the 1925 Worker Olympics were held precisely in Germany under the slogan 'No More War' (although they did actually bar Soviet athletes).

Second, while the IOC Games restricted entry on the basis of sporting ability, the Worker Games invited all comers, putting the accent on mass participation as well as extending events to include poetry and song, plays, artistic displays, political lectures and pageantry.

Third, the IOC Games were criticised for being confined chiefly to the sons of the rich and privileged (through the amateur code and the bourgeois-dominated national Olympic committees). Coubertin himself had always opposed women's participation and readily accepted the cultural superiority of whites over blacks; the two longest-service IOC presidents, Baillet-Labour and Avery Brundage, both collaborated with the Nazi government and were openly anti-Semitic. By contrast, the Workers Olympics were explicitly opposed to all chauvinism, racism, sexism and social exclusiveness; they were truly amateur, organised for the edification and enjoyment of working women and men, and illustrated the fundamental unity of all working people irrespective of colour, creed, or national origin.

Finally, the labour movement did not believe that the Olympic spirit of true amateurism and international understanding could be achieved in a movement dominated by bourgeois–aristocratic leadership. It was therefore determined to retain its cultural and political integrity within the workers' own Olympic movement.

Prague 1921. The first of such international festivals was hosted by the Czechoslovak Worker Gymnastics Association in Prague, 26–9 June 1921, and was advertised as the first unofficial Worker Olympics. It has to be remembered that this event was only three years after the foundation of the nation-state of Czechoslovakia. The festival attracted worker athletes from 13 countries: Austria, Belgium, Britain, Bulgaria, Czechoslovakia, Finland, France, Germany, Poland, Switzerland, the USA, the USSR and Yugoslavia. In addition to sport, the Olympics featured mass artistic displays, choral recitals, political plays and pageants, and culminated in the singing of revolutionary songs.

Frankfurt 1925. The first official Worker Olympics was arranged by the 1.3 million strong Lucerne Sport International in Germany, seven years after the end of the First World War. It was billed by the organisers as a festival of peace. As a British representative put it, if wars are won on the playing fields of Eton, peace can be won on the democratic sports field of the Worker International Olympiads.

The Winter Games, held in Schreiberhau (now Riesengebirge), attracted contestants from 12 countries, while the summer Frankfurt Games had representatives from 19 countries and over 150,000 spectators. Both winter and summer events included traditional competitive sports like skiing, skating, track and field, gymnastics and wrestling, although the organisers stated their intention of avoiding the quest for records and idolisation of individual 'stars'; all the same, they did not discount top performances and the world record for the women's 100 m relay was broken. But the accent was on mass participation and socialist fellowship. For example, every athlete took part in the opening and closing artistic display; the atmosphere was festive and unashamedly political. The opening ceremonies and victory rituals dispensed with national flags and anthems, featuring instead red flags and revolutionary hymns like the Internationale. The centrepiece of the festival was a mass artistic display accompanied by mass choirs, and featuring the multi-person pyramids and tableaux symbolising labour solidarity and power in the class struggle. It culminated in the dramatic presentation *Struggle for the World (Kampf um die Erde)*, using mass speaking and acting choruses which portrayed sport as a source of strength for the creation of a new world.

Despite the success of the Frankfurt Games, they were marred by continuing rivalry between socialists and communists, and were confined to LSI affiliates, excluding all worker associations belonging to the communist RSI, as well as socialist groups and athletes who had had contacts with RSI members (including those who had been to the USSR or played host to Soviet sport groups). Besides Soviet athletes, they therefore excluded as many as 250,000 Germans and 100,000 Czechoslovakians, some of whom staged counter-demonstrations during the Frankfurt Games.

Moscow 1928. As a counter to both the socialist games of Frankfurt and the bourgeois Olympics of Amsterdam in 1928, the communist sport movement put on the First Worker Spartakiad in Moscow. It was launched on 12 August 1928 by a parade of 30,000 banner- and torch-carrying men and women marching in colourful formation through Moscow's Red Square to Dinamo Stadium (the largest Soviet stadium at the time). Despite the boycott by both socialist and bourgeois sport groups, some 600 workers athletes from 14 countries (15 per cent of the total entry of 4000) were said to have taken part. The foreign athletes came from Algeria, Argentina, Austria, Britain (26 participants), Czechoslovakia, Estonia, Finland, France (32 participants), Germany, Latvia, Norway, Sweden, Switzerland and Uruguay.

The comprehensive sports programme of 21 sports (the bourgeois Olympics of 1928 comprised only 17) covered track and field, gymnastics, swimming, diving, rowing, wrestling, boxing, weight-lifting, fencing, cycling, soccer, basketball and shooting. The standards were not as high as those at the Amsterdam Olympics, though Soviet sources claim that in virtually all events the Spartakiad winners surpassed the records set at the Frankfurt Worker Olympics. Yet the emphasis was not solely on sport; the festival included a variety of pageants and displays, carnivals, mass games, motor-cycle and motor-car rallies, demonstrations of folk-games, folk-music and dancing. In addition, there were poetry readings and mock battles between 'workers of the world' and the 'world bourgeoisie' (in which everyone participated, there being no passive spectator for this 'sports theatre' finale).

The winter counterpart to the Spartakiad took place in late 1928 in Moscow with 636 participants in skiing, speed skating (women and men), biathlon and special ski contests for postal workers, firemen, country people and border guards.

Vienna 1931. Although the social democrats (socialists) had held a Worker Sport Festival at Nuremberg in 1928 (with limited success), their next venture was to represent the zenith of the worker sports movement. The LSI, as sponsor, now had over 2 million members, including 350,000 women (over a sixth of the total) and arranged a festival in winter at Mürzzuschlag and in summer at Vienna that far outdid in spectators, participants and pageantry the 1932 bourgeois Olympics at Lake Placid and Los Angeles.

As the invitation by the Austrian hosts to the Vienna Games announced in German, French, Czech and Esperanto, the programme was to include a children's sport festival, a meeting of the Red Falcon (Sokol) youth group, 220 events in all sports disciplines, Olympic championships, national competitions, friendly matches, city games, a combination run and swim through Vienna, artistic displays, dramatic performances, fireworks, a festive parade and mass exercises.

Some 80,000 worker athletes from 23 countries came to 'Red Vienna', and on the opening day as many as a quarter of a million spectators watched 100,000 men and women parade through the streets to the new stadium constructed by the Viennese socialist government. As many as 65,000 later watched the soccer finals and 12,000 the cycling finals. This time the sports programme and ceremony were more in line with the bourgeois Olympics. An Olympic flame was borne into the stadium (carried from Mount Olympus); each delegation marched into the stadium as a separate nation (though under a red flag); and the sports programme roughly paralleled that of the bourgeois Olympics – though it was open to all irrespective of ability, and thereby demonstrated sport for all.

By design the Vienna Olympiad coincided with the opening of the Fourth Congress of the Socialist International, and it was pointedly noted that, whereas the political International assembled no more than a few hundred delegates, the sport International brought together the ordinary people themselves. Indeed, there was no other element of the labour movement in which popular participation was more manifest: congresses might pass resolutions about proletarian solidarity and revolutionary energy, but worker sport provided practical manifestation of those ideas.

Barcelona 1936 and Antwerp 1937. Alarmed at the popularity and grow-ing strength of the worker sports movement, bourgeois governments stepped up their repressive actions. When communist workers tried to organise a Second Spartakiad in Berlin in 1932, they first ran into visa problems (all Soviet and some other athletes were refused visas to enter Germany) and then, when several hundred worker athletes had managed to reach Berlin, the Games were banned.

Under attack from fascism, the socialists and communists at last came together in a popular front, and jointly organised a third Workers Olympics, scheduled for Barcelona in Republican Spain for 19–26 July 1936. They were to be in opposition to the bourgeois 'Nazi Olympics' held in Berlin a week later. The Catalonia Committee for Workers Sport received promises of attendance from over 1000 French worker athletes (the socialist government of Léon Blum gave equal funds to the Barcelona and Berlin teams), 150 Swiss, 100 Soviet, 60 Belgians, 12 Americans, 6 Canadians, and others. The Spanish Olympic Committee declared that it would boycott Berlin and take part in Barcelona.

But the Third Worker Olympics never took place. On the morning of the scheduled opening ceremony, the Spanish fascists staged their military putsch. Some worker athletes remained in Spain to fight in the International Brigade during the Spanish Civil War, and many who returned (like the Canadians, who included the national high-jump champion Eva Dawes) were banned from sport by their national federations – whilst those athletes who had given the Nazi salute to Hitler in the Berlin Olympic opening ceremony returned as national heroes.

After the abortive Barcelona Games, the communist and socialist coalition rescheduled the Third Worker Olympics for Antwerp in 1937. While the Antwerp Games was not as large as that in Vienna, or as the intended Barcelona Games would probably have been, it did present an imposing display of worker solidarity. Despite the difficulties put in their way by increasingly hostile and fascist regimes, special trains carried an estimated 27,000 worker athletes from 17 countries (including the USSR) to Antwerp – an astonishing achievement in the Europe of 1937. Some 50,000 people filled the stadium on the final day, and the traditional pageant through the city attracted over 200,000.

Following this success, a Fourth Worker Olympics was planned for Helsinki in 1943, but war brought down the curtain on an inspiring period of worker Olympic festivals.

The worker sports movement survived the war, bowed but not defeated. It continues today, although the radically different circumstances of the post-war world inevitably brought changes to the movement. Basically the new role was one of selective co-operation and amalgamation with the national (bourgeois) sport federations and clubs, by contrast with the pre-war separate development. The four largest surviving worker sports organisations are the French Worker Sports and Gymnastics Federation (FSGT) with over 100,000 members, the Finnish Worker Sports Union (TUL) with some 450,000 members, the Hapoel socialist worker sports organisation in Israel, and the Austrian Worker Sports and Cultural Association.

Proletarian sport in Soviet Russia in the 1920s

Just as during the Renaissance the bourgeoisie had developed a substantially new pattern of sport imbued with their values, so it was thought perfectly natural by some after the Russian Revolution that a fundamentally new pattern of recreation would emerge, reflecting the requirements and values of the proletariat and the new socialist state.

The first steps to be taken were by no means obvious, for there was no pattern to follow; the change-over from criticism of capitalist institutions and the sports structure of industrial states to practical action in an 85 per cent peasant, illiterate society in the throes of civil war, however, presented enormous problems and dilemmas.

What of the past was valid and useful? Were the schools of gymnastics inherited from Germany, Scandinavia and the Czech and Slovak lands, as well as the organised sports of Britain and the North America utterly 'bourgeois' and unworthy of a place in the new proletarian order? Could Russian imperial societies and movements like the Boy Scouts and Sokol be adapted to Soviet needs, or should a fresh start be made? Was the bourgeois legacy a cancer that had to be cut from the proletarian body to make it healthy, or could the best of bourgeois practice be adapted to serve the needs of the struggling proletarian state?

These were the types of questions that were being debated, often furiously, in educational circles after the Russian Revolution. Two of the leading parties to the debate were the 'hygienists' and the 'Proletkultists'.

The hygienists

The hygienists sharply contrasted physical culture with competitive sport; to their minds, sport implied competition, games that were potentially injurious to mental and physical health. Such pursuits as weight-lifting, boxing and gymnastics were said to be irrational and dangerous, and encouraged individualist rather than collectivist attitudes and values – and, as such, were contrary to the desired socialist ethic. They frowned upon the 'record-breaking mania' of contemporary sport in the West, and they favoured non-commercialised forms of recreation that dispensed with grandstands and spectators. Doubts were cast on the social value of competitive sport – above all, on attempts to attain top-class results. As a future Soviet President, Kalinin, was to put it: 'Sport is a subsidiary affair and should never become an end in itself, a striving to break records . . . Sport should be subordinate to the tasks of communist education. After all, we are preparing not narrow sportsmen, but citizens of communist construction who should possess first and foremost a broad political outlook and organisational ability as well as strong arms and a good digestive system.'[3]

Opponents of 'sport' charged that it distorted the 'eternal ideals' of physical education, that, instead of being universal, it led to narrow specialisation and was detrimental to health, and encouraged commercialism, demoralisation and professionalism. Competitive sport, it was alleged, diverted attention from the basic aim of providing recreation for the masses; it turned them into passive onlookers.

Not all supporters of the hygienists, however, were opposed to every form of competitive sport. The chairman of the Supreme Council of Physical Culture, Nikolai Semashko, who was himself a doctor and concurrently also People's Commissar for Health, was opposed to restricting physical education to narrow medical confines and to banning competitive games: 'If you keep the populace on the semolina pudding of hygienic gymnastics, physical culture will never gain very wide popularity.'[4] Competitive sport was, he believed, 'the open gate to physical culture . . . It not only strengthens various organs, it helps a person's mental development, teaches him attentiveness, punctuality and precision and grace of movement, it develops the sort of will-power, strength and skill that should distinguish Soviet people.'[5] moreover, although he wrote the following words in 1926 – that is, before the full-scale campaign for 'socialist emulation' had been launched to accompany the industrialisation drive – he clearly anticipated the regime's support for competition: 'Competition should serve ultimately as a means of involving people in building socialism. That is how I look upon competitive sport and competition generally.'[6]

All the same, there were others of the hygienist school who did not share his 'broadmindedness'. Several members of his staff at the Health Commissariat and lecturers at the institutes of physical culture, including the principal of the Moscow State Institute of Physical Culture, A. A. Zigmund, were firmly opposed to many competitive games. Zigmund prepared a list of 'approved' sports which included track and field, swimming and rowing (against oneself and the clock, not against opponents); 'non-approved' sports including boxing, wrestling, soccer and fencing, all of which, by their very nature, implied competition. Furthermore, he rejected the 'use of physical exercise as spectacles for mercenary ends, narrow specialisation and professional "*rekordsmenstvo*" [indulgence in record-setting and record-breaking].[7] Since Zigmund was also chairman of the Scientific and Technical Committee attached to the Supreme Council of Physical Culture, his views carried a good deal of weight. This committee was also responsible for physical education syllabuses in primary and secondary schools: as a specific subject, PE was excluded from most schools, inasmuch as it was felt that it should be 'an integral part of the educational process and not something tacked artificially on to the curriculum'. Zigmund asserted that 'the existence of PE teachers is a sign of pedagogical illiteracy'.[8]

Hygienists dominated the teaching of physical culture at the Petrograd and Moscow institutes; in 1924, in fact, the Moscow Institute was, for a time, renamed the Central State Institute of Physical Culture and Curative Pedology[9] in order to bring it more in line with the hygienists' notion of the role of physical culture in Soviet society. The curriculum contained exclusively medical subjects and 'hygienic gymnastics', spurning games and sports.

One result of pressure from the hygienists was the reduction in the number of sports contests that took place in the first half of the 1920s and the exclusion from those contests that did take place of certain 'harmful' sports. The First Trade-Union Games, in 1925, for example, excluded soccer, boxing, weight-lifting and gymnastics from its programme, even though these were four of the most popular sporting pursuits in the country at the time. Boxing was outlawed in the same year by order of the Leningrad Physical Culture Council.

A change in the fortunes of the hygienist school came with Party intervention in the controversy over physical culture and sport in an elaborate declaration in 1925 which effectively rejected them. Their downfall was partly caused by the changing political climate in the mid-1920s and the alleged connection of some of their leading exponents with Trotsky – whose star had been on the wane since 1924. Thus, in the 'witch hunt' of 'Trotskyists' that occurred at the end of the decade, Dr Zigmund was labelled a Trotsky supporter and removed from all his posts (he subsequently vanished in the purges). A more immediate reason for the demotion by the Party of the hygienists may well have been that it was beginning to see competitive sport (with its record-breaking, individual heroes and spectator potential) as a useful adjunct to its impending industrialisation drive. The strong link in communist states, however, between physical culture and health (physical and mental) has remained to this day.

The Proletkultists

In the sphere of sport, the Proletkultists[10] demanded the complete rejection of competitive sport and all organised sports that derived from bourgeois society, as remnants of the decadent past and emanations of degenerate bourgeois culture. A fresh start had to be made through the 'revolutionary innovation of proletarian physical culture', which would take the form of 'labour gymnastics' and mass displays, pageants and excursions. Gymnasiums and their 'bourgeois' equipment would be replaced by various pieces of apparatus on which young proletarians could practise their 'work movements'.

The Proletkultists, therefore, went much further than the hygienists in condemning all manner of games, sports and gymnastics 'tainted' by bourgeois society. In a book entitled *New Games for New Children* which they had published, the Proletkultists advocated such innovatory games as 'Swelling the Ranks of Children's Communist Groups', 'Rescue from the Imperialists', 'Agitators', 'Helping the Proletarians', and 'Smuggling Revolutionary Literature across the Frontier'.[11]

One such novel proletarian 'event' was staged on Moscow's Sparrow Hills in the summer of 1924 with as many as 6000 participants. The spectacle was called simply 'Indians, British and Reds', India being led by a plumed chieftain (!), Britain by 'Joseph Chamberlain' and the Reds by the 'Chairman of the Revolutionary Military Council' (Trotsky). The plan of events was as follows:[12]

(1) life goes on peacefully in all countries, with people engaging in games and sports: Indians in primitive games, hunting, dancing and fighting; the British pursuing sports [note the negative connotation] and carrying out punitive expeditions; and the Reds simulating work in factories, engaging in proletarian recreation and workers' outdoor fêtes;
(2) the British suddenly attack the Indians and conquer them;
(3) the Reds receive an appeal for help, cross the sea and join the struggle;
(4) the Indians join the Reds and, together, attack the British and defeat them;
(5) victory festivals take place in a new communist world.

Many other such theatrical spectacles were presented and Sparrow Hills became a regular stage for proletarian pageants and mock battles. The Proletkult, while accusing others of 'sportisation' and 'militarisation of sport', was itself accused of a 'theatricalisation of sport'.

Another 'proletarian event' took place in 1927 to mark the Tenth Anniversary of the Revolution and was entitled 'The Pageant of Universal October'; it was intended to portray pictures of world revolution. It was a strict rule that no one should simply be a spectator, but everyone should join in – as British miners, American cowboys, turbaned Indians, Polish cavalry, a religious procession of émigrés, huge Chinese dragons pulling rickshaws, Red Army men, workers and peasants – some 7,000 'performers' in all. The two sides, capitalists and workers, suddenly clash and a radio appeal is made to the workers of the world to come to the class front. Universal October is at hand; one last onslaught on the citadels of capital and the announcement is made: 'Now the red banner is flying over the entire world. Salute the GHQ of world revolution, the Communist International.'[13]

While the hygienists admitted the possibility of the usefulness of some 'bourgeois' sports, the Proletkultists made no such concessions. Thus, the hygienist V. V. Gorinevsky described the game of lawn tennis as 'ideal from the biological standpoint in enhancing harmonious development; I find it hard to say what organs and muscles are not in use in tennis'. The Proletkultist, S. Sysoyev, on the other hand, maintained that this game 'for the white-pants brigade and the bourgeoisie exhibits no comradeship or teamwork – the very qualities that the Russian needs. Tennis is also an expensive summer game . . . It should not and cannot receive as much support in the USSR as other, mass games.'[14]

To many Proletkultists, the recourse to 'bourgeois' institutions such as sports seemed a compromise, a withdrawal from already conquered positions. They might have exerted more influence over the movement if they had had a better-defined programme of proletarian physical culture to take the place of organised sports. As it was, a number of factories introduced 'production gymnastics' for their workers and some trade-union clubs confined their activities to 'regenerative exercises', which tended to turn people, especially the young, away from sport and came in for increasing criticism from the Party. Lenin had earlier admonished the Proletkult movement, pointing out the need to draw on the cultural heritage of the past and to base further development on everything valuable that had been accumulated by humanity up to the Revolution: 'What is important is not the *invention* of a new proletarian culture, but the *development* of the best forms, traditions and results of *existing* culture from a Marxist point of view.'[15] Other critics maintained that there were no such separate entities as bourgeois and proletarian sports; there was, rather, a bourgeois and a proletarian *attitude* to sport, a bourgeois and a proletarian *spirit* of competition. Sporting attainments were, they asserted, necessary for inspiring young people to fresh successes in sport, which were, in some way, a measure of the country's cultural and technical development.

Subsequently, several Proletkultist notions were taken up and incorporated in Soviet sport, while their originators were rejected (and mostly liquidated after 1934). 'Production gymnastics' were, for example, to be taken up on a mass scale with the onset of the First Five-Year Plan in 1928 and are, today, a distinctive feature of Soviet physical education, though their purpose is more utilitarian than aesthetic, more geared to higher productivity than the proletarian bodily perfection that the Proletkultists advocated. Further, the attempted portrayal of proletarian grandeur and a messianic mission in sporting displays, pageants, spartakiads, children's games and even art forms, so favoured by the Proletkultists, is still strong in the USSR today.

Conclusions

The influence of the worker sports movement and the future-oriented Soviet visionaries of the 1920s on communist sport today is not often obvious; though that is not to say that future developments will not return to some of the inspiring socialist experiments embodied in worker sport and the Soviet 1920s. Such developments might also learn from mistakes committed by the forerunners of present-day socialist sport.

There are many reasons why the worker sports movement is so weak today, and why it never captured the support of the majority of the working class throughout its history. One handicap was that worker sports almost always duplicated the establishment of bourgeois sport clubs, federations and Olympics. As long as the older associations remained socially (and sexually and racially) exclusive preserves of the bourgeoisie, this was not particularly significant. But once the workers succeeded in partial democratisation of sport, and once firms, the churches and governments came to realise the considerable potential in sport for social control, this presented a major problem. Worker sports societies rarely had the 'name', amenities, or funds to compete with bourgeois teams, and they were often denied access to public funds and facilities.

Another problem was the media. Coverage of worker sport was normally confined to the worker press and it was deliberately ignored by the bourgeois media altogether. Worker sport was shut out of the people's consciousness. And since only a minority of workers read the socialist press, it is not surprising that only a minority of workers joined the worker sports movement or were prepared to turn their backs on the glamorous bourgeois clubs for the low-status worker sports organisations. In any case, it was common for bourgeois clubs to recruit and 'cream off' the best worker athletes by attractive financial inducements.

Efforts were certainly made to enhance the attractiveness of worker sport, but they were hampered by a number of problems: the explicitly political nature of worker sport, the uncertain and at times insensitive attitude to organised sport and competition by labour leaders, and the tactical differences over the role of sport in society, not to mention the social–democrat communist wrangling. What many worker sports leaders seem to have failed to understand was that a sports organisation might be *more* politically effective by being *less* explicitly political.

An early hindrance to the popularity of worker sport was the theoretical argument over the role of sport in society. At one extreme were the Soviet Proletarian Culture advocates and their supporters in countries like Sweden, who saw (bourgeois) sport as a reflection of degenerate bourgeois culture that had to be totally rejected since it was permeated by chauvinism, exploitation and militarism; what was needed was a new proletarian system of physical culture based on personal fulfilment, mutual respect and solidarity. At the other extreme were those like many British and North American socialists who regarded sport as one's personal affair, on the periphery of superstructural phenomena and therefore relatively apolitical, not something for the labour movement to 'waste' scarce resources on. Typically, both extremes resulted in the weakest of all the worker sports movements in the industrial world.

Where the worker sports movement did flourish, it was not without internal problems. In the early years the focus was on non-competitive participation, but as the 1920s and 1930s wore on the bourgeois obsession with records, spectators and victory (at all costs) tended to infiltrate worker sport, which increasingly featured an element of competition. It is not uncommon today, indeed, for socialist and communist newspapers to devote the bulk of their sports coverage to horse-racing and winning forecasts!

The worker sports movement needed to expand if it was to fulfil its cultural and political mission. But the needs of growth presented complex problems. Organised sport, like the working class itself, is a product of modern industrial capitalism, and in a bourgeois world a large proportion of working women and men is steeped in bourgeois values. None the less, it has to be said that, notwithstanding, the worker sports movement did try to provide an alternative experience based on the workers' own culture and inspired by visions of a new and exciting socialist culture. To this end it organised the best sporting programme it could, regardless of the level – whether a Sunday bike ride over the moors or a worker olympic festival – based on truly socialist values. Its history is not only an essential part of labour history, it is an integral component of the story of world sport that is all too often totally ignored by historians.

On the other hand, the years of experimenting and searching in the USSR in the 1920s reflect a contradiction fundamental to the period: that between the subjective desires to shape society according to ideological preconceptions and the objective lack of the material conditions for implementing ideals. There can be little doubt that, because they were not based on the reality of Soviet Russia's circumstances, some immediate aspirations, including those of the hygienists and Proletkultists, were utopian and unrealistic. Even so, the questions they raised are fundamentally important and relevant to any assessment of the role and functions of sport in society.

Were they to pass judgement on contemporary sport, they would surely be critical of much Western sport for being tied to the profit motive, seeing it as something to package up and sell, as well as a distraction for the populace, a new opiate of the people, all of a piece with the Hollywood dream factory and the sex–scandal–sport tittle-tattle of much of the mass media, selling a vicarious and largely fantastical experience and thereby helping to ensure conformity with the consensual status quo of capitalist society.

But they might wonder, too, how it has come about that the present-day communist sports system supports such an elaborate system of government sports departments, sports boarding schools, giant amphitheatres, coaches, semi- and full-time professional players, sports journalists, and so on – even gambling establishments; and wonder why a similar sports ideology in East and West cultivates irrational loyalties and ascribes similar prominence to the winning of victories, the setting of records, and the collecting of medals and trophies. Might they still wonder whether sport should exist under communism?

Notes

1 V. I. Lenin, *Leninsky sbornik*, vol. 35 (Politizdat, Moscow, 1945), p. 148.
2 For a full account of the worker sports movement in 16 countries, see Arnd Krüger and James Riordan (eds), *Der internationale Arbeitersport* (Pahl-Rugenstein, Cologne, 1985). See also James Riordan, 'Worker sport – a socialist alternative', in Gary Whannel and Alan Tomlinson (eds), *The Five-Ring Circus* (Pluto Press, London, 1984).
3 Mikhail Kalinin, *O kommunisticheskom vospitanii* (Moscow, 1962), p. 17.
4 Nikolai Semashko, 'Fizicheskaya kultura i zdravookhranenie v SSR', in *Izbrannye proizvedeniya* (Moscow, 1954), p. 264.
5 *Ibid.*

6 Nikolai Semashko, *Puti sovetskoi fizkultury* (Moscow, 1926), p. 22.
7 A. A. Zigmund, *Izvestiya fizicheskoi kultury*, no. 22, 1925, p. 2.
8 A. A. Zigmund, *Vestnik fizicheskoi kultury*, no. 3, 1925, p. 2.
9 Pedology, which was widely practised in the 1920s, was considered to be the science of child development, using experimental and observational techniques and taking into account both heriditary and environmental factors. In their published views on sport some pedologists claimed that certain sports were harmful and encouraged selfish habits. In 1936 Stalin declared pedology a 'pseudo-science' and proscribed its practice and teaching.
10 The Proletkult (abbreviation for 'Proletarian Cultural and Educational Organisations') was formed in 1917 with the intention of producing a proletarian culture as an indispensable part of a socialist revolution. It became widely influential after the Revolution, but was abolished by the Party in 1932.
11 M. A. Kornileva-Radina and Y. P. Radin, *Novym detyam – novye igry* (Moscow, 1927), p. 37.
12 Z. Starovoitova, *Polpred zdorovya* (Moscow, 1969), pp. 139–40.
13 *Ibid*.
14 'Diskussiya o laun-tennise', *Krasny sport*, 21 January 1924, p. 3.
15 V. I. Lenin, *Leninsky sbornik*, vol. 35 (Moscow, 1945), p. 148.

Chapter Four
Sport and modernising communities

So much attention in the West has focused on leading communist states as successful sporting nations that we have often failed to notice a far more influential role of communist sport – as a medium of social change. This radically distinguishes it from the part played by sport in Western development. It is a role common to that played by sport in many modernising societies which include, we must remember, most communist states, especially China, Cuba and the USSR.

The unique pattern of Western sport and our discussions on sport are no more than a mirror of our own societies. In countries of scarcity, societies striving to build a new life for mainly illiterate, starving, impoverished peasant populations, Western commercialised sports on the one hand, and the gentlemanly 'sport for sport's sake' ethos on the other, are often looked upon as irrelevant, if not immoral.

Sport in modernising communities is a serious business with key functions to perform. It is accordingly state-controlled, encouraged and shaped by utilitarian and ideological designs (it is by no means a matter merely of fun and games). In its development it is associated with health, hygiene, defence, patriotism, integration, productivity, international recognition, even cultural identity and nation-building. Sport frequently has the quite revolutionary role of being an agent of social change, with the state as pilot. In any case, after liberation there is rarely a leisure class around to promote sport for its own personal enjoyment.

Many developing states stress the idea that physical is as vital as mental culture in human development, and that it should be treated as such both for the all-round development of the individual and, ultimately, for the health of the society. In the classic treatment of this issue back in 1917, Mao Zedong actually placed physical culture *before* mental culture:

> Physical culture is the complement of virtue and wisdom. In terms of priorities, it is the body that contains knowledge, and knowledge is the seat of

virtue. So it follows that first attention should be given to a child's physical needs; there is time later to cultivate morality and wisdom.[1]

Mao here is echoing the Marxist philosophy (see above) of the inter-dependence of the mental and physical states of human beings.

Sport, or rather physical culture, evidently has particular social significance in the development of modernising societies. This is all the more so because the place of sport is more central in their social systems. The study of sport in centrally planned and socialist-governed societies may therefore be singularly revealing, inasmuch as it deals with such a wide range of social processes and investigable forms of activity within which a whole nexus of social phenomena has found fairly open expression.

The following would seem to be the main state priorities assigned to sport in modernising societies.

Nation-building

All developing nations face problems of political stabilisation, economic–social–cultural progress, and national integration of eth-nically diverse populations. A major problem is that of nation-building: the inculcation of political loyalties to the nation as a whole, transcending the bounds of kinship, race, language, religion and geo-graphical location.

Not only is this a key policy in post-revolutionary Russia, China and Cuba, it is equally relevant to post-liberation countries in Africa and Asia. After all, as a Nigerian has said of Africa,

> Nations were carved out and created by colonial masters in the 19th and early 20th centuries, in some cases so arbitrarily that peoples were either separated or brought together with other peoples of completely different origin and background. Consequently, one finds that many African nations are, even now, still in search of true national identities.[2]

What better than sport to help them find those identities? After all, sport, with its broad relevance to education, health, culture and politics, and its capacity to mobilise people (predispose them towards change), may uniquely serve the purpose of nation-building and help foster national integration. It extends to and unites wider sections of the population than probably any other social activity. It is easily under-stood and enjoyed, cutting across social, economic, educational, ethnic, religious and language barriers. It permits some emotional release (reasonably) safely, it can be relatively cheap and is easily adapted to support educational, health and social welfare objectives.

And it is here that the sports introduced mainly by Westerners at the turn of the century (in, say, China, Russia, Cuba and other developing states) may have some advantages over indigenous folk-games in that the latter are often linked to festivals which mainly take place annually in the various communities. Indigenous sports have therefore served only as a means of expressing tribal or ethnic identity. Modern sports have served as an important means of expressing national identity.

Integration

Bound up with nation-building is the state-desired aim of integrating a multinational population, often in transition from a rural to an urban way of life, into the new nation-state. Many modernising societies are loose confederations of diverse ethnic groups: different colours, languages, traditions, religions, stages of economic growth, prejudices.

Let us take the world's three largest populations.

The 1000 million people of China consist of at least a dozen distinctly different ethnic groups; the country is divided into 21 provinces and 5 ethnic autonomous regions. The minorities constitute aborigines (Chuan, Yi, Maio, Manchu, Puyi) and Koreans in the east; Mongols, Turks (Uighurs) and Tibetans in the west.

India's 750 million people constitute three major linguistic groups (Hindi, Urdu and Punjabi accounts for 46%) and dozens of other groups: Telugu 10%, Tamil 8%, Marathi 8%, Bengali 8%, Gujarati 5%, Kanarese 4.5%, Oriya 3%, Malayalam 3%, Assamese 1%, in addition to Kashmiri and British.

The USSR is certainly not Russia; it is a multinational federation of over 280 million people containing over a hundred nationalities. The country is divided into 15 Union Republics, each based on a separate ethnic group, and many other administrative subdivisions (autonomous republics, autonomous regions, territories and national areas). Every weekday children learn in as many as 87 different languages and daily newspapers come out in 64 languages. Russians actually comprise less than half the total population today.

The governments of all three of these great nations have quite deliberately taken Western sports from town to country and, in the case of the USSR from the European metropolis to the Asiatic interior, and used them to help integrate the diverse peoples into the new nation and to promote a patriotism that transcends petty nations and ethnic affiliation.

In Soviet history, even before the Civil War was over, the new Soviet regime organised the First Central Asian Games in the old Islamic centre of Tashkent in October 1920. This was actually the first time in history that Uzbeks, Kazakhs, Turkmenians, Tadjiks, Kirkghiz and other Muslim peoples, as well as Russians, Ukrainians and sundry Europeans, had competed in any sporting events together. As was made clear later, 'The integrative functions of sport are enormous. This has great importance for our multinational state. Sports contests, festivals, spartakiads and other forms of sports competition have played a key role in cementing the friendship of Soviet peoples.'[3]

In China, similarly, the ethnic games festival held in Beijing in September–October 1985 was 'designed to help integrate the diverse peoples of the state: in this case a rather subtle kind of integration, for it appeared to be predicated on assertions of ethnic difference, but conducive nonetheless to integration in the framework of the socialist state and legitimation of nationality policies'.[4]

As we shall see below, the integrating functions of sport are just as clearly evident when the competitive elements are added: in the case of the USSR these seem to have become very important from the end of the 1920s, in China only from the late 1970s. Both internally and externally sport is used to mobilise people in ways which actively contribute to the raising of group consciousness and solidarity, goals explicitly favoured by leaders.

Defence

Since many modernising states (especially in Africa and Asia) were born in war and today live under the constant threat of war, terrorism and subversion (e.g. Nicaragua, Cuba, Afghanistan), it is hardly surprising that defence is a prime consideration; sport is therefore often subordinated to the role of military training. In some countries the system is best described as a 'militarisation of sport'. The role of the military in sport is further heightened by centralised control of sports development. Even before their revolutions, however, China and Russia had military personnel playing a prominent role in sports administration largely because of their countries' geopolitical situation and history of foreign invasion. It has to be remembered that both countries have extensive borders with foreign states – 14 for China, 12 for the USSR. And, even in recent times both countries have lost unimaginable numbers of people in wars. For example, China lost 13 million and the USSR 27 million in the Second World War, far and away the greatest human war losses in world history.

In China, the USSR and several Asian and African states, the sports movement was initially the responsibility of the armed forces and even today is frequently dominated by instrumental defence needs and military or paramilitary organisations. Most developing nations, for example, have a nation-wide fitness programme with a bias towards military training, often modelled on the Soviet GTO system. In China, as two North American scholars attest,

> A major component of physical culture in Chinese schools is the military preparation program based on the Soviet GTO system. Route marches of 10 to 20 kilometers, grenade throwing, dashes, mock and real rifle training form the core of this program.[5]

Even in a relatively industrially advanced country like the GDR, albeit a European 'front-line state', it was the Soviet military-oriented fitness system that was pursued:

> The performance objectives of the sport and physical educational programmes are based on the requirements of a graded sports badge, the pattern of which was adopted from the Soviet Union . . . Initially this badge carried the imposing title of 'Ready to Work and Defend Peace' and was heavy with militaristic and ideological requirements . . . [it has since become] 'Ready to Work and Defend the Homeland'.[6]

All communist and some non-aligned states have a strong military presence in the sports movement through armed and security forces' clubs, provide military sinecures for more-or-less full-time athletes and, at times, have established direct military supervision over sport and physical education, such as in the USSR in the periods 1918–22 and 1940–46. They are also linked through the Sports Committee of Friendly Armies, set up in Moscow in 1958 (see below pp. 126–47).

In many developing states, therefore, particularly in the communist community, the armed and security forces provide many of the funds and facilities that enable people to take up and pursue a sport, especially full-time and in sports involving expensive equipment (ice hockey, soccer, gymnastics, weight-lifting and equestrianism). They thereby help to ensure that as many people as possible are physically fit, mentally alert and possess the qualities (patriotism, will-power, stamina, ingenuity) that are regarded as being of particular value for military preparedness (and for internal policing against dissidents and deviants). Furthermore, military organisation of sport appears to be an efficient way of deploying scarce resources in the most economical fashion and using methods of direction that are more effective coming from paramilitary than from civilian organisations.

Health and hygiene

Of all the functions of state-run sport in modernising societies, that to promote and maintain health must take priority. In many such states sport comes under the aegis of the health ministry. In so far as sports development has been based for much of the Soviet period on a population at a comparatively low health level, and as it has served as a model for several other modernising societies, it will be instructive to examine briefly that experience. Of course, post-revolutionary Soviet Russia was not as backward as are some African and Asian nations today, but the country was among the world's poor nations (10 million starved to death in 1921, for example), had recently been a semi-colony and received virtually no aid from without.

When the Russian communists took power in October 1917 they inherited a semi-feudal, 80 per cent peasant and illiterate empire of over 100 different ethnic groups. The country was in a state of war-ruin and chaos, it was a land with an overwhelmingly inclement climate, where disease, epidemics and starvation were common, and where most people had only a rudimentary knowledge of hygiene. The new rulers well knew it would take a radical economic and social transformation to alter the situation significantly. But time was short, and able-bodied and disciplined men and women were needed urgently, first for the country's survival, then for its recovery from the ravages of war and revolution, its industrial and cultural development, and its defence against further probable-seeming attacks.

Regular participation in physical exercise, therefore, was to be one means – relatively inexpensive and effective – of improving health standards rapidly and a channel by which to educate people in hygiene, nutrition and exercise. And for this purpose a new approach to health and recreation was sought. The name given to the new system was *physical culture*.

The pre-revolutionary and Western conception of sport and physical education was thought to be too narrow to express the far-reaching aims of the cultural (mental and physical) revolution under way. Physical culture was to embrace health, physical education, competitive sport, and even civil defence and artistic expression. The acquisition of that culture was said to be an integral process that accompanied a person throughout life.

As Nikolai Semashko, himself a doctor and the first Health Minister (also concurrently Chairman of the Supreme Council of Physical Culture), made plain shortly after 1917,

> Physical culture in the Soviet understanding of the term is concerned not with record breaking, but with people's physical health. It is an integral part of the cultural revolution and therefore has personal and social hygiene as its major objective, teaching people to use the natural forces of nature – the sun, air and water – the best proletarian doctors.[7]

In other words, physical culture was to be a plank in the health campaign, encouraging people to wash, to clean their teeth, to eat and drink sensibly, to employ a rational daily regime of work, rest and sleep (hence Semashko's slogan of 'Physical Culture 24 Hours a Day' – eight hours' work, eight hours' sleep and eight hours' recreation[8]). Even more than that: the country was in the grip of a typhoid epidemic, had long suffered from such near-epidemic diseases as cholera, leprosy, tuberculosis and venereal disease; it suffered, according to Semashko, from 'dreadfully backward sanitary conditions, the ignorance and non-observance of rules for personal and public hygiene, leading to mass epidemics of social diseases such as syphilis, trachoma, scabies and other skin infections'.[9]

Physical culture, therefore, was to help combat serious disease and epidemics. The therapeutic value of regular exercise, for example, was widely advertised in the intermittent anti-TB campaign of the late 1920s. But physical culture was not confined to improving *physical* health; it was regarded as important in combating what the leaders defined as anti-social behaviour in town and country. If young people could be persuaded to take up sport and engage in regular exercise, they might develop healthy bodies *and* minds. Thus, the Ukrainian Party issued a resolution in 1926, expressing the hope that 'physical culture would become the vehicle of the new life . . . a means of isolating young people from the baneful influence of the street, home-made alcohol and prostitution'.[10] The role assigned to physical culture in the countryside was even more ambitious: it was

> to play a big part in the campaign against drunkenness and uncouth behaviour by attracting village youth to more sensible and cultured activities . . . In the fight to transform the village, physical culture is to be a vehicle of

the new way of life in all measures undertaken by the authorities – in the campaign against religion and natural calamities.'[11]

And in the 1980s, the name of sport was still being invoked to combat alcoholism and religion.[12]

Physical culture, then, stood for 'clean living', progress, good health and rationality, and was regarded by the authorities as one of the most suitable and effective instruments for implementing their social policies, as well as for the *social control* implicit in the programme. It was to be the 'handmaiden of Soviet medicine' and, in Semashko's oft-repeated dictum, 'there can be no physical culture without medical supervision'. This was to 'symbolise the bond between medicine and Soviet physical culture'.[13]

As industrialisation got under way at the end of the 1920s, physical exercise also became an adjunct, like everything else, of the Five-Year Plan. At all workplaces throughout the country a regime of therapeutic gymnastics was introduced with the intention of boosting productivity, cutting down absenteeism through sickness and injury, reducing fatigue, and spreading hygienic habits among the millions of new workers who had only recently inhabited bug-infested wooden huts in the villages.

There is no space here to go into greater detail of the development of health-related sport in the USSR. Suffice it to say that the nation has come a long way since 1917: from educating peasants in the virtues of washing and cleaning their teeth; from preaching the virtues of *mens sana in corpore sano* to illiterate and starving people (from nomadic Kazakhs to maritime Inuit, from Siberian tribes to Muslim peoples in Soviet Central Asia, from the Slavs to the Caucasians); from dealing with epidemiology, hygiene and nutrition; to providing the foundation of the country's progress to becoming the world's most successful all-round sporting nation. It is, regretfully, the latter that has taken the West's attention; yet it is the former which is of far more relevance to modernising countries everywhere.

Social policies

There are many facets of social policy relevant to sport that concern developing states. Some have been referred to above: combating crime, particularly juvenile delinquency, combating alcoholism and prostitution, attracting young people away from religion (especially all-embracing faiths like Islam that impinge on large segments of social life). [One aspect of the use of sport for social purposes is the concern that it can make some contribution to the social emancipation of women.] And here the international example of women's increasing sports participation and success, especially by non-Europeans, can affect women in those developing countries of Africa, Asia and Latin America in which women have traditionally been discouraged (or banned) from pursuing a sport.

[A strong motivation here can be the desire by leaders for national recognition through international sports success. The attention paid by some East European nations to women's sport has sometimes contrasted strongly with the relative neglect in both the more 'enlightened' nations of the West and in developing states. As a GDR sports official has noted, 'While other nations can produce men's teams as good as if not better than ours, we beat them overall because they are not tapping the potential of their women.'[14]]

It would seem to be mounting Western official (as well as Western women's) awareness of losing out to communist nations that has contributed to encouraging, *inter alia*, heightened interest in women's sport and the training methods for women employed in Eastern Europe. But the influence is sometimes the other way. For example, it was the US women's example that encouraged Chinese women to take up weight-lifting and body-building (and even boxing), so that in May 1985, '140 musclewomen in 23 teams from all over the country took part in the Jinan tournament'.[15] Developing countries also owe much of their success in international sports competitions to their female athletes (as in the case of South Korea in the 1986 Asian Games and the 1988 Summer Olympics – in which it took fourth place in the medals table).

The impact of women's sport is even greater – though emancipation is far more protracted and painful – in communities in which women have, by law or convention, been excluded from public life and discouraged from baring face, arms and legs in public. In fact, some multi-ethnic communities have quite deliberately used sport to break down prejudice and gain a measure of emancipation for women. This has been a conscious policy in communist nations with a sizeable Muslim population, like Albania, the USSR and, latterly, Afghanistan. In a reference to women of Soviet Central Asia (bordering on Iran, Turkey and Afghanistan), a Soviet sports official has asserted that 'sport has become an effective and visible means of combating religious prejudice and reactionary tradition; it has helped to destroy the spiritual oppression of women and to establish a new way of life'.[16] It is a sobering thought that had the grandmothers of such Soviet Uzbek gymnasts as Nelli Kim or Elvira Saadi appeared in public clad only in a leotard, they would almost certainly have been stoned to death – as, indeed, would women today in some fundamentalist Islamic societies.

Significantly, it took until 1980 for the first-ever Black woman athlete to win an Olympic field event – Cuba's María Colon in the javelin. And in 1984, two women athletes from India and Morocco were the first women from their respective countries to reach Olympic track finals, with the Moroccan winning a gold medal.

Change can be painfully slow, but inasmuch as women's sporting attainments are reflecting, reinforcing and even *precipitating* processes of social change in the role and status of women, this clearly offers exciting prospects for the future of women in modernising societies.

International recognition and prestige

For young countries trying to establish themselves in the world as nations to be respected, even recognised, sport may uniquely offer them an opportunity to take the limelight in the full glare of world publicity. This is particularly important for those nations confronted by bullying, humiliation, boycott and subversion from big powers in economic, military, political and other areas. As Fidel Castro has said of imperialist states in regard to Latin America, 'Imperialism has tried to humiliate Latin American countries, has tried to instil an inferiority complex in them; that is part of the imperialists' ideology to present themselves as superior. And they have used sport for that purpose.[17]

This puts particular responsibility on athletes from developing nations in that they are seen by political leaders as encouraging a sense of pride in their team, nationality, country, or even political system. The patriotic pride generated by sports success, especially against the world's strongest nations, further helps to integrate ethnically diverse societies. It is for these reasons that sport is often treated with such reverence in so many developing societies. Even the poorest of them – such as Ethiopia – seeking to use it for nation-building, and in the process so flagrantly contradict our Western ideas about 'sport for sport's sake', about what they ought to be doing with their meagre resources.

It is an irony that at a time when some in the Western metropoles are casting doubt on Western sports in their competitive and commodified form, including in the Olympic Games (which some see as having become too big, too nationalistic, too political and too commercialised), some governments of modernising societies, first and foremost communist governments, are among the strongest defenders of the faith – of Western sports and the Olympics.

We shall deal in more detail with the role that sport plays in communist foreign policy in Chapter 8.

Some conclusions

To Westerners accustomed on the one hand to the notion of sport for sport's sake, a private garden of human activities, and on the other hand of sport for profit, professional entertainment measured in both millions of dollars, sport in developing states will come as a revelation. In economies of scarcity, a massive social force like sport cannot be excused responsibility, cannot be allowed to be merely a means of escape (important as that sometimes is). And while it may sometimes be proper to defend the freedom of sport (say, from bureaucratic state manipulation), let us be careful not to give it a status more important than life itself.

Precisely because sport is potentially such an immense social force, it is evidently far too important to be permitted to develop haphazardly, or left to the whim of private clubs, businessmen, circus promoters and rich foreigners – as it was in virtually all modernising countries before their national liberation and regeneration.

The state control and planning of sport in such modernising communities as Cuba, Nicaragua, China, the Soviet Union and even Ethiopia may well have more relevance to developing nations than will our own experience of sports development. That said, it is equally clear that Western sports and organisations do have a vital role to play in Africa, Asia and Latin America – though it has to be a responsible one. This can only happen, however, when the 'First World' stops trying to make Third World sport merely an appendage of its own system.

That sport is germane to developing, especially communist, countries and to their social change would seem beyond dispute. What *kind* of sport is a matter for debate. Perhaps a mixture of indigenous games and Western sports modified and adapted to suit local conditions and national culture? But without state support to promote and protect a nation's cultural identity, the latter can trample upon the young shoots of the former – or even emasculate them and package them up for mass consumption and profit, as has happened with some popular games and pastimes in Western societies (e.g. darts, snooker, bowls, even 'fun runs').

One thing is certain: far from being a luxury, sport or, better still, *physical culture*, appears to be a vital necessity in modernising societies.

Notes

1 Mao Zedong, *Une étude de l'éducation physique* (Maison des sciences de l'homme, Paris, 1962; originally published in Chinese in 1917).
2 H. E. O. Adefope, 'The role of sport in the creation of national identity', in *Sport in the Modern World* (Springer, New York, 1973), p. 567.
3 V. V. Rodionov, 'Sport i integratsiya', *Teoriya i praktika fizicheskoi kultury*, no. 9, 1975, p. 7.
4 Chris Hann, *'The withering of muscular socialism: physical culture, nutrition and personal responsibility in contemporary China'* (unpublished paper: May 1987), p. 3.
5 Robert G. Glassford and Roy A. Clumpner, 'Physical culture inside the People's Republic of China', *Physical Education around the World*, Monograph 6 (1973), p. 13.
6 David Childs, 'Sport and physical education in the GDR', in James Riordan (ed.), *Sport under Communism* (Hurst, London, 1978), p. 78.
7 Nikolai Semashko, 'Desyatiletie sovetskoi meditsiny i fizicheskaya kultura', Teoriya i praktika fizicheskoi kultury, no. 5, 1928, p. 3.
8 Nikolai Semashko, *Puti sovetskoi fizkultury* (Fizkultura i sport, Moscow, 1926), p. 37.
9 Semashko, 'Desyatiletie sovetskoi meditsiny . . .', p. 2.
10 A. M. Landar, 'Fizicheskaya kultura – sostavnaya chast kulturnoi revolyutsii na Ukraine', *Teoriya i praktika fizicheskoi kultury*, no. 12, 1972, p. 11.
11 *Ibid.*, p. 13.
12 See V. P. Nekrasov, 'Fizicheskaya kultura protiv pyanstva', *Teoriya i praktika fizicheskoi kultury*, no. 9, 1985, pp. 37–9; B. A. Lisitsyn, *Sport i religioznye organizatsii* (Fizkultura i sport, Moscow 1985); and P.S. Stepovoi, *Sport. Politika. Ideologiya* (Fizkultura i sport, Moscow, 1985).
13 Nikolai Semashko, 'Desyatiletie sovetskoi meditsiny . . .', p. 9.
14 See *Teorie und Praxis der Körperkultur*, no. 3, 1976, p. 74.
15 Z. Wubin, 'A rising sport in China', *China Sports*, no. 9, 1985, p. 5.
16 R. Davletshina, 'Sport i zhenshchiny', *Teoriya i praktika fizicheskoi kultury*, no. 3, 1976, p. 62.
17 Fidel Castro quoted in S. Castanes (ed.), *Fidel. Sobre el deporte* (El Deporte, Havana, 1974), p. 290.

Chapter Five
Sport and the state

Two distinguishing features of the communist sports system are its central organisation and its employment for specific socio-political objectives. This contrasts with Western sports administration which runs the gamut from almost anarchic diffusion of agencies involved in sport (Britain) to structures strongly influenced by commercial concerns (Italy, USA). However, in communist countries like China and the USSR sport has traditionally been centrally controlled and fully integrated into the polity. Sport and politics are inseparable. The policy of the sports governing body has invariably been determined by the ruling party and it is the party that has appointed the sports committee/ministry/secretariat. Sometimes, as was recently the case of the GDR Sports Secretariat Chairman, Manfred Ewald, the Chairman/Minister was concurrently a member of the ruling Politburo.

It follows that all sports federations are ultimately dependent upon and guided by the government, even though most world ruling sports bodies contain regulations that, like those of FIFA, 'exclude any national association that permits government bodies to interfere in its activities'.[1] Similarly, in communist states the national Olympic committees (NOC) are, contrary to IOC regulations, government agencies appointed by the government-controlled sports committee. Any decision on participation in the Olympic Games, therefore, is made by the ruling party leadership, often without consultation with the NOC or even the sports committee. As happened over the widespread communist boycott of the Los Angeles Olympics in 1984, the decision was simply passed down for implementation. The world governing bodies for sport, including the IOC, evidently turn a blind eye to the flagrant violation of their charters.

Priorities once established, the system of central planning and control sees to it that all levels co-operate in carrying out government sports policy – from central to local government, from enterprise management to trade unions, from the armed forces to schools and colleges, from recreation officers to coaches. The advantages of such a centrally planned system lie mainly in efficiency and consistency, an ability to concentrate resources on government-decided priorities, like Olympic success. The disadvantages arise largely in tendencies towards bureaucracy and lack of initiative and independent enterprise. All the thousands of volunteers who give their time free to Western sport as sports officials, medical advisers and youth club administrators tend to have no equivalents in communist sport.

On the other hand, state administration of sport provides ample opportunities for far-reaching bureaucracy in every area of sporting life. The USSR Sports Committee, for example, employs 448 people who earn a well-above-average living from sport: 557 roubles a month for top officials, 454 for executives and 400 for the rest – some two or three times the average Soviet salary. Altogether, the Soviet Union has several thousand state-run sports organisations up and down the country, including 95 academic and research institutions, 390 sports schools, 55 training camps and 26 industrial enterprises, employing almost 100,000 people. The various sports committees alone employ 8000 people.[2] This vast army of civil servants, employed specifically in sport, may well have a vested interest in retaining the status quo; indeed, their livelihoods depend upon it. Like state-run sports organisations the world over, they represent a conservative body resistant to change.

Since sports organisation in communist states comes under government direction, it is perhaps understandable that the sports movement has been set explicitly utilitarian functions – primarily for work and military training, for the all-round development of the model citizen, and for the pursuit of certain foreign-policy goals. These goals have naturally varied over time and between states.

An authority on GDR sport describes the distinguishing features of its (recent) sports system as follows:

A party system which makes possible consistent planning over a prolonged period; A unifying central body which embraces every aspect of sport; State support at the highest level of policy making; A sports system which, because of the above factors, is loyal to, and completely integrated into, the political system of the country; The utilisation of sport as an agency of national prestige in return for which the State recognises and rewards sporting achievement; A dependence on and cooperation with the USSR in sport no less than in other areas.[3]

The last factor applied to a number of other communist countries, though none as strongly as the GDR, before the breaching of the Berlin Wall.

The reasons for this 'politicisation' of sport, which parallels sports development in many modernising societies, have to be sought in the enhanced role of sport as a social institution and part of the cultural revolution in communist societies.

Structure and organisation

Overall direction of the communist sports movement is provided by a Sports Committee attached to the government; this is the umbrella organisation for all other elements in the sports movement: the various sports societies and clubs, the individual sports federations, the nation-wide fitness programme, the sports rankings system, the sports schools, coaching, competitions, research, and sports medicine and science. This structure can be seen in Figures 2 and 3 for the USSR and GDR respectively, which also demonstrate the near-identical nature of their sports organisation.

Figure 2 *Administrative structure of Soviet sport*

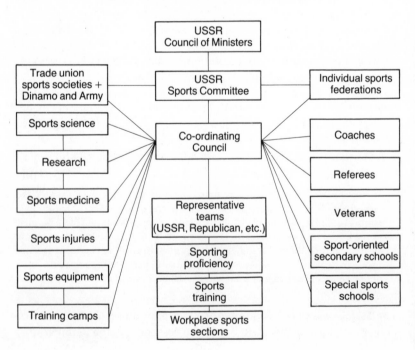

Figure 3 *Administrative structure of GDR sport*

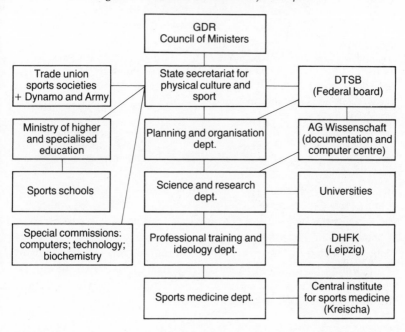

The sports movements in the USSR and GDR have, until recently, been administered by the Committee on Physical Culture and Sport and the State Secretariat on Physical Culture and Sport respectively. While these administrative agencies have determined overall policy for sport, the executive bodies have largely been the trade unions, with their nation-wide sports societies financed and run by the parent trade union. Once again, it is the Soviet structure that has tended to set the tone for other 'fraternal' countries to follow, as Figures 2 and 3 and Table 1 show in the case of the USSR and GDR.

Each sports society and club has its own rules, membership cards, badge and colours. The trade union sports societies are financed out of trade union dues: a 1% levy is put on each union member; approximately a quarter of trade union funds go to sport; Dinamo/Dynamo and CASC/ Vorwärts are financed out of security forces and army funds. Each society and club has responsibility for building sports amenities, acquiring equipment for its members, and maintaining permanent bodies of coaches, instructors, medical personnel and maintenance

Table 1 *Major sports societies and clubs in the USSR and GDR*

USSR	GDR	Group represented
Burevestnik	Wissenschaft	Students
Lokomotiv	Lokomotive	Railway employees
Vodnik	Hansa	Ship workers
Spartak	Einheit	Municipal employees
The two non-trade-union sports clubs are:		
Dinamo	Dynamo	Security forces and general public
Central Army Sports Club	Vorwärts	Armed forces and general public

staff. All members have the right to use their society's facilities for a nominal fee. Contests are arranged between sports societies and clubs, each society has its local and nation-wide championships for each sport it practises, and its teams play against teams representing other sports clubs and societies. There therefore exist nation-wide leagues and cup competitions in a whole range of popular sports, such as soccer, basketball, volleyball and ice hockey. Each club or society has teams of full-time professionals in every major town.

The role of the armed and security forces

Sport and the military are associated in varying degrees during the development of virtually all societies. The link would appear to be particularly close in modernising societies which progress in a comparatively brief historical span from a way of life which has recently been largely traditionalist. This is apparent today in a number of African and Asian states, but it is nowhere so pronounced as in the communist countries.

All communist states have a strong military presence in the sports movement through army and security forces clubs, and provide military sinecures for full-time athletes. Since many of these military features were copied from the USSR, it will be instructive to see how the link between the military and sport was forged in Soviet development.

Interestingly enough, the 'militarisation' of sport in the Soviet Union was not a creature of communist development; it was already well advanced in the Russian Empire. In 1912, following tsarist Russia's poor showing in the Stockholm Olympic Games (Russia took 15th place), the tsarist government appointed General Voyeikov as Chief Supervisor of the Physical Development of the Population of the Russian Empire; he was, in effect, the first state minister for sport with control over all sports and quasi-sports organisations in the country. Three years later his office was inherited by the Bolsheviks following the November 1917 Revolution and transformed into the military-training organisation known as Vsevobuch. Once the new regime had prevailed in the Civil War and repelled the foreign intervention in the country, Vsevobuch handed over the reins of sport in 1923 to the Health Ministry. Vsevobuch meanwhile became the sports club of the Central House of the Red Army, based in Moscow. When the Red Army was renamed the Soviet Army following the Second World War (during which time sport once again became the direct concern of the armed forces), the sports club acquired its present name of Central Sports Club of the Army (TsSKA). Nowadays, TsSKA is the largest of the sports organisations run by the Soviet Army, Navy and Air Force, which have a sports club (*sportivny klub armii* – SKA) in every military district.

These clubs of the armed forces provide amenities both for servicemen (as part of compulsory military service and for 'regulars') and also for the general public. So, because an athlete is a member of an army sports club (or of Dinamo – see below), it does not follow that he (or she) is automatically a serving man or woman. For example, many Soviet ice-hockey and soccer players, most full-time gymnasts, figure-skaters, cyclists, show-jumpers, boxers, weight-lifters, water-polo players, rowers, scullers and yachtsmen are members of the army sports club or Dinamo because of the expensive amenities and equipment needed to practise these sports.

For many full-time athletes and coaches, the army provides the wherewithal to enable them to gain access to the best facilities and financial security. It also enables them to retain their 'amateur' status in international sport. Dinamo was founded as a sports club on 24 June 1923 on the initiative of Felix Dzerzhinsky, then head of the internal security agency, the Cheka (which became successively the GPU, OGPU, NKVD, MVD, MGB and KGB); membership was initially confined to service personnel of the internal security agency, border guards and internal troops, as well as members of their families.

In a relatively short time the society had sections in almost every sizeable town in the country. Being the first of the great Soviet sports societies and with the security agency's resources behind it, it was able to command substantial sports facilities, including the first of the Soviet Union's big new sports stadiums, the Dinamo Stadium on Leningrad

Prospect in the north of Moscow, which was the country's largest until the opening of the Lenin Stadium on the Moscow River in the south-west of the city in 1956. Today Dinamo is still the wealthiest and most powerful of all Soviet sports societies.

Until the glasnost period, inaugurated in 1985, official censorship prevented mention of Dinamo's link with the security forces, even though it had long since opened its doors to the general public, often with the utilitarian aim of encouraging the cultivation of activities of a direct or indirect paramilitary nature. With their considerable resources and tentacular organisation, it is hardly surprising that the Soviet security forces should also have a strong influence upon the sports organisations of young people within the USSR and of several states in Eastern Europe and elsewhere.

In all communist states, the army and security forces therefore provide many of the funds and facilities which enable people to take up and pursue a sport; they thereby help to ensure that as many people as possible are physically fit, mentally alert and possess the qualities (patriotism, will-power, stamina and ingenuity) that are said to be of particular value for military preparedness.

In linking sport ideologically and even organisationally with military preparedness, the USSR and several other communist states seem to have been motivated by the following factors:

(i) a fear of war and a conviction of the need to keep the public primed to meet it;

(ii) the all-pervasive presence throughout society of the military and security forces, necessitated by the imposition from above, should enthusiasm from below flag, of 'socialist construction' upon the public;

(iii) the policy of keeping the public in a state of controlled tension, ready to tolerate the discipline and sacrifice necessitated by socialist transformation and, in the case of most communist states, of rapid industrialisation, and ready to conform to the standards set by the leaders and to acquiesce in their policies;

(iv) given the fairly lukewarm attitudes towards physical exercise in most modernising societies (typical of all peasant or recently peasant communities) and few sports amenities for the general public, military organisation of sport has been an efficient method of deploying scarce resources in the most economical way and using methods of direction which have probably been more effective coming from paramilitary than from civilian organisations.

Nation-wide fitness programme

Every communist country has a nation-wide fitness programme based on that practised in the Soviet Union, the 'Prepared for Work and Defence' (*Gotov k trudu i oborone* –/GTO). It is through this programme that most people take part in sport, and it is regarded as the foundation of the entire communist sports system. The target is not excellence in a single sport, nor even general skills, but all-round ability in a number of events and knowledge of hygiene, first aid and civil defence, for which token gold and silver badges are awarded. Its objective is to make physical exercise a regular feature of everyday life and to extend the scope of sports participation, giving everyone something to aim for – that is, to set modest targets whose attainment brings some honorific recognition. In some countries, this programme is the basis of the school physical education curriculum. Thus, in the USSR the upgraded GTO programme (1972–85) 'became the basis of Soviet physical education in terms of syllabus and qualifying standards'.[4]

Planning quotas in respect of this programme are set for every club, society, region, school and college, and tests are held throughout the year. The main concern of most sports clubs is, in fact, to see that members obtain their fitness programme badges.

The motives behind the programme would seem to include the following:

(i) to attract children into regular physical exercise and sport at an early age, partly because it is felt that the earlier they become engaged in sport and keeping fit, the more likelihood there is of their taking part in sporting activity later on, and partly because, to ensure international sporting success, it is increasingly necessary to spot and nurture giftedness at an early age;

(ii) the programme is used for direct military training: a civil defence test, grenade throwing, rifle shooting and gas-mask training are to be found at several stages of the programme;

(iii) to cut down absenteeism from work through illness by making workers physically and mentally more fit (through physical training and sport) to cope with the changing techniques of industry and farming – and thereby raising productivity;

(iv) to attempt to channel the zest and energy of young people into relatively healthy recreation, particularly in urban environments where leisure time is increasing.

In a speech to launch the revised GTO programme in 1972, the then Soviet sports minister Sergei Pavlov made most of these points:

> The GTO should be employed to organise people's leisure time more rationally, to improve public health and prevent industrial disease, to combat misuse of increasing spare time, to tighten work and public discipline, and to improve educative work among young people.[5]

In the Soviet Union the 'Be Prepared for Work and Defence' (*Bud gotov k trudu i oborone*) and 'Prepared for Work and Defence' (*Gotov k trudu i oborone*) programmes came into being in the 1930s (the former in 1934, the latter in 1931). Although no credit has ever been given to Baden Powell's Boy Scout movement, the fitness programme was based, as its name 'Be Prepared' implies, on standards set for the 'marksman' and 'athlete' badges, as prescribed in Baden Powell's book *Scouting for Boys*.[6] The 'Be Prepared' programme existed between 1934 and 1972 for schoolchildren, covering 16 different sports and theoretical subjects.

The GTO programme is normally updated every ten years on average. The standards set in the USSR in 1985 consisted of the following:

Seven age-stages:
I   6–9-year-olds
II   10–11-year-olds
III 12–13-year-olds
IV   14–15-year-olds
V   16–17-year-olds
VI   18–39-year-olds (with four age-groups: 18–24; 25–29; 30–34; 35–39)
VII 40–60 men (with four age-groups: 40–44; 45–49; 50–54; 55–60)
     40–55 women (with three age-groups: 40–44; 45–49; 50–55)

Men over 60 and women over 55 may also take stage VII with doctor's permission. See the Appendix to this chapter for the full programme of stages I to VI.

Each stage consists of two sections. The first, theoretical, part consists of a knowledge of physical culture (history, structure, aims) and international sport; of personal and public hygiene (knowing the effect of exercise on the organism; the rudiments of first aid; the ill effects of smoking, taking alcohol and drugs; self-control through regularly checking weight, sleep, diet, pulse, breathing); and of civil defence. Boys aged 16–18 (the pre-conscript age), for example, have to undergo an initial military training programme, while 16–18-year-old girls (girls do not do army service) have to learn the basic rules of civil defence (including wearing a gas mask for an hour in a gas chamber).

The second, practical, part of the GTO programme involves exercises that promote physical qualities like speed, stamina, strength and skill, as with running for speed and stamina, jumping for height and length, throwing, skiing, swimming and weight-lifting (boys only). Stages IV–VI also include hand-grenade throwing and shooting. The practical norms for stage IV, for example, are based on track and field, gymnastics, skiing and skating (cycling or cross-country running in snow-free regions), swimming, shooting, outdoor pursuits and orienteering; all 16–18-year-olds are also expected to achieve a set (higher) standard or ranking in the sport of their choice.

To sum up, in varying degrees much of the public in communist countries has been able to pursue a sport or engage in physical recreation, using facilities mostly free of charge through the trade unions or an army or Dinamo club. But it has been difficult for casual enthusiasts to take up the sport of their choice owing to the lack of amenities open to the general public and the confining of most sports clubs and schools to the 'gifted'. This may have opened up 'elite' sports like yachting and equestrianism to people from all walks of life who have shown natural ability and inclination; but it has also meant a concentration of resources on the privileged few.

Moreover, the coercive and plan-fulfilment nature of physical activities available to the public at large – as with the 'production gymnastics' at the workplace, the national fitness programme, and the compulsory recreation lessons for students – may have brought schoolchildren, students and servicemen into functional recreation, yet it has undoubtedly built up a resistance and resentment in regard to diktat, to the privileged few who have access to scarce resources, and even to sport itself.

It is noteworthy that one of the first actions of the newly liberated regimes in Eastern Europe after 1989 has been to abandon the Soviet GTO; indeed, there are signs that it is being quietly discontinued in the Soviet Union itself (see Chapter 9).

The communist authorities have not permitted sport to develop haphazardly, in the hands of individual enthusiasts, as it had in Anglo-Saxon states especially. Sport in China, Cuba, Vietnam and the USSR has not been, as it once was, left to the whim of foreigners, commercial promoters, circus entrepreneurs, or private clubs with restricted entrance. It has been shaped and run by the state as an adjunct to the state's economic, political and social policies.

This system may well have produced world-beaters and healthier, more productive workers and better defenders of the country. For decades, however, this only strengthened authoritarian elements in society. Success in high-performance sport was purchased at the expense of sport for all. The physical and moral health of the nation actually suffered as a result. As the recent transformation of Soviet and Chinese sport shows, the new mood seems to reflect the rise of Western-style individualism within the realm of physical culture and popular culture as a whole.

Appendix

USSR National Fitness Programme (1985)

Vsesoyuzny fizkulturny kompleks 'Gotov k trudu i oborone SSSR' (All-Union Physical Culture Programme 'Prepared for Work and Defence of the USSR')

Introduced in 1931
New version 1985

I   6–9-year-olds
II   10–11-year-olds
III 12–13-year-olds
IV   14–15-year-olds
V   16–17-year-olds
VI   18–39-year-olds (with four age-groups: 18–24, 25–29, 30–34 and 35–39)
VII 40–60 men (with four age-groups: 40–44, 45–49, 50–54 and 55–60)
     40–55 women (with three age-groups: 40–44, 45–49 and 50–55)
     Men over 60 and women over 55 may also take stage VII
     Personnel of the armed forces have their own Military Sports Programme.

Stage I 'Ready for the start' 6–9-year-olds

General knowledge
Importance of physical culture for health. The hygienic and tempering importance of washing, rub-down and bathing. Choosing dress and footwear for
games, walks and exercise.

Skills
To perform free gymnastic exercises.

Weekly motor requirements

	Girls	Boys
Running [or skiing] (km)	7–9 [8–10]	8–10 [10–12]
Skipping (no. of times)	800–1000	800–1000
Chin-ups on high bar	–	20–25
or pull-ups on low bar	45–50	45–55
or push-ups	45–50	45–50
Leg raising from horiz. posn.	50–60	50–60
Forward bend, legs straight	50–60	50–60

Tests and standards

	Girls		Boys	
	Pass	Gold badge	Pass	Gold badge
3 × 10 m run (sec)	9.8	9.1	10.4	9.6
or high start 30 m run	6.2	5.7	6.3	5.8
1500 m run		any time allowed		
Jumps, 8 (m)	9	12.5	8.8	12.1
Ball throwing at target from 6 m, from five throws (target)	3	4	3	4
Chin-ups on high bar	2	4	–	–
or pull-ups on low bar	–	–	8	13
Skiing 1 km [2 km] (min, sec)	8.30	8.00	9.00	8.30
	[any time]		[any time]	
Swimming, any time (m)	25	25	25	25

Stage II 'All start' 10–11-year-olds

General knowledge
Role of physical culture in improving health and school performance. Health rules of doing exercises. Rules for morning exercises and exercise breaks at schools. Breathing during exercises.
Civil defence programme.

Skills
To perform exercise break programme.
To know civil defence programme.

Weekly motor requirements

	Boys	Girls
Running [skiing] (km)	10–12 [12–14]	9–11 [10–12]
Skipping (no. of times)	1000–1200	1000–1200
Chin-ups on high bar	30–35	–
or pull-ups on low bar	55–70	50–60
or push-ups	55–70	50–60
Leg raising from horiz. posn.	70–80	60–70
Forward bend, legs straight	60–70	60–70

Tests and standards

	Boys		Girls	
	Pass	Gold badge	Pass	Gold badge
60 m run (sec)	10.6	10.0	10.8	10.4
2000 m run		any time allowed		
Long jump (cm)	300	340	260	300
or high jump (cm)	100	110	95	105
Ball throwing, 150 g (m)	27	34	17	21
Chin-ups on high bar	4	6	–	–
or pull-ups on low bar	–	–	10	15
Skiing 1 km (min, sec)	7.00	6.30	7.30	7.00
or 2 km	25	any time	allowed	
Untimed swimming (m)	3	50	25	50
Rifle shooting (hits, points)		30	3	27

Stage III 'Bold and skilful' 12–13-year-olds

General knowledge
Importance of exercise for enhancing mental and physical capacity. Exercises in
school regime. Eating and drinking when engaging in PE and sport. Safety
regulations for exercises.
Civil defence programme.

Skills
To perform morning exercises and exercise break programme.
To know the civil defence programme.

Weekly motor requirements

	Boys	Girls
Running [skiing] (km)	12–14 [14–16]	10–12 [12–14]
Skipping (no. of times)	1300–1500	1300–1500
Chin-ups on high bar	35–45	–
or pull-ups on low bar	70–85	60–70
or push-ups	70–85	60–70
Leg raising from horiz. posn.	90–100	80–90
Forward bend, legs straight	70–90	70–90

Tests and standards

	Boys		Girls	
	Pass	Gold badge	Pass	Gold badge
60 m run (sec)	10.2	9.4	10.4	9.8
1500 m (min, sec)	7.30	7.00	8.00	7.30
or 2000 m		any time allowed		
Long jump (cm)	350	380	300	350
or high jump (cm)	115	125	100	110
Ball throwing, 150 g (m)	31	39	19	26
Chin-ups on high bar	5	8	–	–
or pull-ups on low bar	–	–	15	19
Skiing 2 km (min, sec)	14.00	13.00	14.30	14.00
or skiing 3 km		any time allowed		
50 m swimming (min, sec)	any time	0.50	any time	1.07
Rifle shooting (hits, points)	4	34	3	32
Cross-country hike		day-long 5–6 km		

Stage IV 'Sporting reserve' 14–15-year-olds

General knowledge
Self-control in exercising. Objective and subjective indicators of self-control. Major methods of tempering organism. Tempering effects of sport. Harmfulness of smoking and drinking for engaging in sport.
Civil defence programme.

Skills
To take one's pulse when exercising. To know the civil defence programme.

Weekly motor requirements

	Boys	Girls
Running [or skiing] (km)	13–15 [16–18]	11–13 [14–16]
Skipping (no. of times)	1500–1800	1500–1800
Chin-ups on high bar	45–55	–
or pull-ups on low bar	–	70–85
or push-ups	85–100	80–85
Leg raising from horiz. posn.	100–120	90–100
Forward bend, legs straight	90–100	90–100

Tests and standards

	Boys		Girls	
	Pass	Gold badge	Pass	Gold badge
60 m run (sec)	9.2	8.4	10.0	9.4
2000 m run (min, sec)	10.00	9.20	12.00	10.20
		any time allowed		
or 3000 m run	380	430	330	370
Long jump	125	130	110	115
or high jump (cm)	40	45	23	26
Ball throwing, 150 g (m)	8	10	–	–
Chin-ups on high bar	–	–	15	20
Sit-ups with hands behind head	18.00	17.30	20.00	19.30
Skiing 3 km (min, sec)		any time allowed		
or 5 km	any time	0.43	any time	1.05
50 m swimming (min, sec)	4	33	4	32
Small-bore rifle shooting, 25 m	3	32	3	30
or 50 m (hits, points)	4	34	3	32
or pneumatic rifle				
Cross-country hike		day long 12 km		

Stage V 'Strength and courage' 16–17-year-olds

General knowledge
Fatigue, over-fatigue and over-training, warning signs and treatment. Taking pulse and training load in exercising.
Civil defence programme.

Skills
To use self-control indicators in exercising. To apply first aid to sports injuries. To hold competitions for the various *GTO* events. To know the civil defence programme.

Weekly motor requirements

	Boys	Girls
Running (km)	15–17	12–14
or skiing (km)	20–22	16–18
Skipping (no. of times)	1800–2000	1800–2000
Chin-ups on high bar	60–70	–
or pull-ups on low bar	–	80–95
or push-ups	100–120	100–120
Leg raising from horiz. posn.	120–140	100–120
Forward bend, legs straight	90–120	90–100

Tests and standards

	Boys		Girls	
	Pass	Gold badge	Pass	Gold badge
100 m run (sec)	14.5	14.2	16.5	16.0
2000 m run (min, sec)	–	–	11.30	10.00
or 3000 m (min, sec)	15.00	13.00	–	–
or any time allowed (m)	5000	5000	3000	3000
Long jump (cm)	420	460	340	380
or high jump (cm)	130	135	115	120
Hand-grenade throwing, 700 g (m)	32	38	–	–
Hand-grenade throwing, 500 g (m)	–	–	18	23
Downward circles on high bar	3	4	–	–
or chin ups on bar	10	12	–	–
Sit-ups with hands behind head	–	–	20	25
Skiing 3 km (min, sec)	–	–	19.00	18.30
5 km (min, sec)	27.00	25.00	–	–
or any time allowed (km)	10	10	5	5
50 m swimming (min, sec)	any time	0.41	any time	1.00
Small-bore rifle shooting (25m)	4	37	4	35
or 500 m (hits, points)	4	35	4	32
Cross-country hike or orienteering	day-long 20–25 km			

Sport, politics and communism

Stage VI 'Physical perfection' 18–39-year-olds

General knowledge
Optimum motor regime for people of various occupations. Independent exercising methods, such as limbering up, exercise breaks at work, jogging and walking etc. Taking pulse and loading in exercising depending on sex, age, state of health and physical fitness. Rational diet and exercise as important factors in fortifying health and improving work capacity.
Massage as a means of restoring the organism after physical loading.
Civil defence knowledge.

Skills
To perform 'production gymnastics' with account for specific work or future occupation. To do basic self-massage. To perform civil defence programme.

Weekly motor requirements

	Age (years)			
	18–24	25–29	30–34	35–39
	Men			
Jogging (km)	15–17	21–25	21–25	21–25
or skiing (km)	22–24	30–35	30–35	30–35
Chin-ups on high bar	70–85	50–60	50–60	50–60
or push-ups	120–140	250–300	200–250	200–250
Raising straight legs from horiz. position	140–160	210–250	180–210	180–210
Hike (rapid walking) (km)	–	–	21–35	21–35
Forward bend, legs straight	90–120	70–100	–	–
	Women			
Running (km)	12–14	15–20	15–20	15–20
or skiing (km)	16–18	16–18	12–15	12–15
Jumping with or without rope	350	350	210–250	210–250
Push-ups on bench or chair	210–220	210–220	150–170	150–170
or pull-ups	85–95	80–85	65–70	65–70
Sit-ups with hands behind heads	100–120	210–220	160–170	160–170
Forward bend, legs straight	90–100	49–56	35–49	35–49
Hike (rapid walking) (km)	21–35	21–35	25–40	25–40

Test and standards

	18–24		25–29		30–34		35–39	
	Pass	Gold badge	Pass	Gold badge	Pass	Gold badge	Pass	Gold badge
Men								
100 m run (sec)	14.3	13.5	14.6	13.9	—	–	–	–
3000 m run (min, sec)	13.2	11.4	13.5	12.1	14.2	12.5	14.4	13.1
or 5000 m			any time allowed (ata)					
Grenade throwing, 700 g	38	46	36	42	33	36	32	35
Chin-ups on high bar	9	11	7	10	6	9	5	8
5 km skiing (min, sec)	25.3	23.3	26.0	24.0	27.0	26.0	29.0	27.0
or 10 km (min)	54	50	53	51	55	53	60	56
or any time allowed (km)	15	15	15	15	15	15	15	15
50 m swimming (sec)	ata	0.42	ata	0.43	ata	0.45	ata	0.46
Small-bore rifle shooting								
at 25 m (hits, points)	4	42	4	42	4	40	4	40
or at 50 m	4	38	4	38	4	36	4	36
Hike or orienteering			day-long 20 km for all age-groups					
Women								
100 m run (sec)	17.0	15.7	17.5	16.5	–	–	–	–
2000 m run (min, sec)	11.4	10.3	12.0	11.3	12.3	12.0	12.3	12.0
or 3000 m			any time allowed (ata)					
Grenade throwing, 500 g (m)	22	27	20	25	18	23	17	21
Sit-ups with hands behind head	40	50	40	50	35	45	30	40
Skiing 3 km (min)	19	17	20	18	21	19	22	20
or 5 km (min)	35	31	36	32	37	33	38	34
or any time allowed (km)	10	10	10	10	10	10	10	10
50 m swimming (min, sec)	ata	1.11	ata	1.14	ata	1.20	ata	1.23
Small-bore rifle shooting								
at 25 m (hits, points)	4	38	4	38	4	36	4	36
or at 50 m (hits, points)	4	36	4	36	4	34	4	34
Hike or orienteering			day-long 20 km					

Translated from *Fizicheskaya kultura v shkole*, no. 7, 1985, pp. 17–27.

Notes

1 A Soviet publication comments quite openly on this violation of the rules in calling for more independence of Soviet federations. See 'Footballers versus officials', *Soviet Weekly*, no. 52, 25 December 1988, p. 15.
2 Nikolai Rusak, 'Medali ili zdorovye?', *Argumenty i fakty*, 28 April 1–4 May 1990, p. 7.
3 See Peter Sutcliffe, 'Sport in the German Democratic Republic', unpublished Ph.D. Thesis, University of Bradford, 1988, p. 327.
4 V. M. Kachashkin, *Metodika fizicheskovo vospitaniya* (Fizkultura i sport, Moscow, 1972), p. 54.

5 Sergei Pavlov, 'Novy kompleks GTO', *Sovetsky sport*, 27 February 1972, p. 2.
6 The similarity is clear if one compares the standards set for the 1931 Soviet 'Be Prepared for Work and Defence' programme with the 'marksman' and 'athlete' badge standards set in *Scouting for Boys* (Pearson, London, 1926), pp. 37 and 43.

Chapter Six
Provision for giftedness

In provision for giftedness, a number of communist countries would seem to have demonstrated that the highest realisation of human potential can be most effectively achieved through the planned application of society's resources; they have attained this goal in a range of fields of excellence and their achievements have generally been inspired by the notion that giftedness can and should be identified early and nurtured both for the benefit of individual self-fulfilment and for the enjoyment and pride that the community gains from the application of that talent.

This appears to be so not simply in sport, but in musicianship, ballet, art and mathematics as well. There is clearly a strong belief that the culture of the body is as vital as that of the mind for the harmonious development of the individual and, ultimately, for the health of society. This belief in the parity of physical and mental culture in human development comes from a conviction that giftedness in physical culture should be treated no differently from talent in mental culture. In other words, a budding gymnast or figure-skater should be given as much opportunity to develop her or his gifts as are promising ballet dancers or violinists.

This contrasts with the conventional Western approach of leaving talent development generally to the physical, moral and financial resources of the individual, and the stigma attached to the cultivation of sports excellence. Of all the disciplines accorded special education for the gifted in the leading communist nations, sport is the most endowed. For not only does it possess the largest number of residential schools, it has the most developed system of talent identification, testing and nurturing that far surpasses anything devoted to ballet, music, art, or the sciences. In the GDR and USSR, for example, the number of sports boarding schools (27 and 40 respectively) exceeded all other residential schools for the gifted taken together.

The reasons for this bias towards sports talent development have to be sought, as well as in the philosophy outlined above, in a number of other factors. First, communist sport follows foreign policy and has cardinal functions to discharge. These functions include winning support for the nation and its communist ideology among developing states; gaining recognition and prestige in the world generally; demonstrating the advantages of the socialist way of life; and gaining internal support for a government that can achieve such international success. Second, athletes are held in high esteem for the skill, grace and strength by which they inspire young and old to be active and join in at all levels of sport. They also help to instil a pride in one's team, nationality and country, and even in the political system that can produce such world-beaters. That is why it is so important for sports personalities to be both exemplary, an inspiration to all, and ambassadors of goodwill and models of propriety in the arenas and forums of the world. Finally, unlike the early administrators of amateur sport in the West, the communist leadership has never been constrained by the notion that sport is an unworthy profession or career.

Olympic success and communist development

The success of the policy of sports talent development is patently apparent if we examine communist participation in the Olympic Games.

When communist nations made their debut in numbers at the 1952 Summer Olympics in Helsinki, they won 29% of the medals; by 1972 they had won 47%; 1976 well over half (57%); and in 1988 they won 64%. In the more than three decades since their debut at the summer Olympics the communist nations have consistently provided six of the top ten countries in the Olympic medal tables.

In the summer Olympics the German Democratic Republic advanced from 15th medal place in 1956 to 2nd in 1976 and again in 1988, overtaking the USA; and in the winter Olympics from 16th in 1956 to 1st in 1980 and again in 1984, overtaking the USSR. The GDR had fewer than 17 million people and was considerably poorer economically than the most advanced Western nations.

Socialist Cuba improved from 53rd in the unofficial points total on its summer Olympic debut in 1960 to 23rd in 1972, 8th in 1976, and 4th in 1980 (it boycotted the 1984 and 1988 Olympics). In the last more-or-less normal Olympics in which it competed, in 1976, it won more medals (13) than the rest of the other 30 Latin American states put together (10). And at the successive Pan-American Games held in the 1980s, it won more gold medals than Canada and the rest of Latin America combined, being placed second only to the USA. Cuba had a population of 9 million in 1980.

Although China competed in the 1932, 1936 and 1948 Olympic Games (before the Revolution in 1949), it won no medals at all. When it renewed its Olympic membership and competed in the Los Angeles Olympics in 1984 it took 4th place, winning 15 gold, 8 silver and 9 bronze medals. China also won the Asian Games of 1986 and 1990.

The Soviet Union has 'won' every Olympics, summer and winter, for which it has entered, with the sole exception of 1968, and the winters of 1980 and 1984. It won a quarter of all the medals at the Seoul Olympics in 1988. The USSR is also the most versatile nation in Olympic history, competing in all summer and winter sports, and winning medals in 21 of the 23 sports represented at the 1988 Olympics.

Western nations do have compensations in some world sports, such as soccer, tennis and basketball, although even there communist athletes and teams are rapidly catching up.

The rankings pyramid

Although it would be misleading to imagine that a uniformly applied programme of rankings, tests and standards is employed to select, grade and forecast sporting talent, the leading communist states do have carefully planned guidelines to spot potential talent and guide performers to take up the sport they are most likely to do well in. This overall programme has been largely based on that employed in the USSR, although several nations have adjusted it to their own conditions and provided innovations which the USSR and others have since taken up (e.g. sports boarding schools). We have seen above that each communist state has a nation-wide programme of physical fitness based on the Soviet 'Prepared for Work and Defence' system. Besides involving as many people as possible in regular physical exercise, this programme aims at establishing a mass base from which potentially gifted athletes can be drawn. Once they are discovered they have to be categorised according to level of ability in a particular sport and given the incentive and amenities to realise that potential. For this purpose a uniform rankings system exists for individual sports, setting various levels of superior achievement.

Although the first communist rankings system came into being in the USSR in 1935, the idea of such a system was by no means new or confined to communist countries. A multi-rankings system existed in Germany from the time of the Weimar Republic; it was refined and extended to cover all major sports during the Nazi era. In Russia, four nation-wide rankings had existed for track and field athletes in 1918, for cyclists in 1924, for swimmers in 1927 and for gymnasts in 1934. An even higher honorary title, Merited Master of Sport of the USSR, came into existence in 1934; two years later this 'Merited' title was applied to other fields too: Merited Artist and Merited Teacher. Along with the title went an increment in the recipient's monthly salary – 10 roubles in the case of teachers and 20 roubles in the case of athletes. As far as sport was concerned, 1st, 2nd and 3rd rankings and Master of Sport existed by 1937 in ten sports; boxing, fencing, gymnastics, shooting, speed skating, swimming, tennis, track and field, weight-lifting and wrestling. The Master of Sport title was awarded to athletes setting good nation-wide records, winning a major Soviet championship or gaining the 1st ranking in a few sports. The practical effect of this new system was to stratify in sport, to distinguish a professional group of athletes from the main body. The fact was that once an athlete reached Master level he or she could devote time and energy full-time to sport.

This rankings system was copied by China in the late 1930s, along with several other features of the Soviet sports system, and by all other communist states following the Second World War. As standards rose and the international commitment of communist, especially Soviet, states grew, two new sports rankings were introduced, in 1965: International Class Master of Sport and Candidate Master of Sport. Meanwhile, all rankings standards were revised once every four to five years in line with rising international and national standards. Figure 4 shows the current rankings and titles pyramid of the Soviet Union.

Merited Master of Sport of the USSR is a state honorific decoration outside the classification system. It is awarded to outstanding athletes who achieve success in major international tournaments. A monthly 'premium' goes with the award.

International Class Master of Sport of the USSR is awarded for international success either in sports in the Olympic programme, world or European championships, or (in certain sports) in other important international championships (e.g. Wimbledon for tennis players).

Master of Sport of the USSR is awarded for international success or for exceptional domestic results in a particular sport.

Candidate Master of Sport of the USSR is a sort of probationary award before the athlete meets the targets of Master of Sport. Its importance lies

Figure 4 *Sports rankings and titles in the USSR*

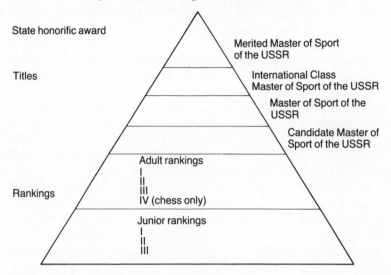

in the fact that it is the Master standard at which athletes can become professionals.

In chess and draughts, the title *Grand Master of the USSR* is the equivalent of International Class Master of Sport of the USSR for other sports. The USSR also awards the title *Master of Folk Sport* for those who meet certain standards in folk-games.

Sports rankings I–IV are awarded for results achieved in official competition within the USSR (nation-wide championships, leagues, cups and spartakiads) and are valid for two years only, after which time they either lapse or have to be renewed – or, of course, the athlete may try for a higher ranking. To obtain a second or third ranking the athlete must also have satisfied the requirements of the GTO fitness programme for that particular age category. Junior rankings are awarded to athletes up to 18 years of age who have also met the qualifying standards of the appropriate GTO programme for their age.

The qualifying standards for each category are high and are revised regularly to keep pace with changing world standards. In some sports (for example, swimming and running) the athlete competes against the clock; in others the rankings may depend on the number of victories gained in contests with athletes of equivalent or higher rankings. In boxing, for example, the 1988 classifications stipulated that to become an

International Class Master of Sport, the contender had to be among the first eight in the Olympics or World Championships. To gain a second adult ranking, a boxer must have eight victories in a year against third-ranked boxers. Each ranking has to be renewed every year by gaining three victories over boxers in the ranking immediately below.

In team games, victories in regular league and cup games count. For example, for the third basketball ranking a player must be a member of a team that has won no fewer than seven matches during a year against teams of any qualification in a national league, as long as the player has made at least 14 appearances for the team.

The physical token of having gained one of the rankings is a badge and a certificate awarded by the Sports Committee. Master of Sport and higher titles earn the athlete an additional 50–100 roubles a month (about a quarter to half of the average Soviet monthly industrial earnings) paid by the USSR Sports Committee. All ranked and titled athletes gain certain rights: to take part in official competitions; to receive preferential treatment in applications for admission to sports schools and colleges of physical culture. They also have prescribed duties: to conduct themselves in accordance with the sporting code of ethics, to pass on their expertise and experience to others, to improve their cultural and political standards, to compete on behalf of their clubs, and constantly to submit to medical supervision.

Any violation of these obligations may result in the loss of the title or ranking – a not infrequent occurrence. In recent years a number of soccer and ice-hockey players have been deprived of their awards for receiving illegal payments, for taking part in 'fixed' matches, or for behaving badly in public or during matches. Naturally, any defecting athlete automatically forfeits all domestic rankings and titles. Leading athletes and coaches are expected to be models of good behaviour at all times.

Talent seeking

The search for talent in sport in the leading communist nations has been based on a centrally planned (and, especially in the GDR, computer-assisted) system of selecting, testing, grading and sifting over a long period. The overall approach to talent identification tends to focus on establishing a model for each sport and event. This is made up of statistical data from a large number of domestic and foreign world-class athletes in the particular sport. It includes information on performance at various ages, the rate of progress, and the ideal physical profile. The planners are thus able to set approximate standards for what can be expected from a potentially gifted athlete at a certain biological age.

From a collation of over a hundred Soviet and GDR studies of talent selection and forecasting, the data used can be said typically to include the following:

anthropological measurements (height, weight, arm reach);

general physical performance (speed, strength, power, endurance, mobility, agility);

performance levels in particular sports (swimming, sprinting, long jump, etc.);

sport-event-specific performance ability for example, in track and field:

100 and 200 m – speed endurance

400 to 1500 m – aerobic and anaerobic endurance

3000 to 10,000 m – aerobic endurance

hurdles – speed, speed endurance, mobility, agility jumps – power, speed

throws – power, strength;

rate of progress in these indicators.

Once a model has been created for a sport, the relevant standards and anticipated rate of progress are used to select potential talent in *three* major stages over four or five years. The age at which the youngster is involved in the system depends on the sport, ranging from 7–8 in swimming, gymnastics, tennis and figure-skating to 12–13 in boxing and cycling, and 13–14 in shooting and weight-lifting.

Stage 1: basic selection

This takes place either at school during the PE lesson or at the various non-residential sports schools. Since the PE lesson is fairly uniform throughout the country, it is relatively easy to measure potential talent at this point. The main standards observed at this stage normally include height and weight; speed (30 m from standing start); endurance (12–15-minute run); work capacity (step tests); power (standing long jump); and sport-specific tests for performance level and technique efficiency.

Stage 2: preliminary selection

This occurs some 18 months after Stage 1. Assessment is based on a number of factors: progress made in physical ability and the sport-specific tests, rate of physical growth, biological age, psychological aptitude, and so on. At this stage it is usual to guide youngsters towards a particular sport or group of sports. There has been some reluctance in the USSR and China, though less in the GDR and Romania, to specialise early, on the grounds that the rates of motor development tend to be erratic.

Some youngsters are eliminated after the preliminary selection has been made, but they will be given another chance to prove their worth a year later when they are reassessed. Those found suitable in the second assessment will join the training squads at the sports schools until the final selection takes place.

Stage 3: final selection
This occurs about three or four years after Stage 1, usually at age 13–14, depending on the sport. For example, in most track and field events it is felt that, on average, 12–14 for boys and 11–13 for girls are the best ages to make performance predictions so as to guide youngsters towards a particular event. Based once more on the ideal model parameters of a particular sport, the final selection takes account of:

standards attained in a specific sport (e.g. times and distances in run-
    ning, jumping, throwing);
rate of progress in sport;
stability of performance (how often good performances occur);
results of physical capacity tests;
results of event/sport-specific performance capacity tests;
results of psychology tests;
anthropometric measurements (e.g. height for basketball, arm-reach for
    discus, agility for gymnastics).

Once the person is identified as possessing potential talent, he or she will normally be offered a place at a residential sports school. It is, none the less, evident from the literature that a number of problems constantly exercise the minds of coaches and medical specialists who plan these schedules. One problem is the lack of satisfactory evidence to separate *true* from *apparent* potential. Young people may attain a high standard of test results at a certain age, yet fail to reach the forecast performance. This problem is underlined by the high drop-out/rejection rate at sports schools; over half of those selected in the early stages of talent identification for sports schools do not attain the anticipated performance levels. A second problem is the varying rates of progress in physical performance indicators, with surges in some at certain ages and relatively slow development in others. Some research findings show that such unstable progress occurs in speed and power between 12 and 15, in muscle endurance between 14 and 15 and between 16 and 17, in strength between 13 and 16, and in endurance between 12 and 14.

Thirdly, there is still much disagreement about the most suitable age at which to commence sport-specific training. Youngsters often display good all-round ability in the 10–12 age-group, and there appear to be dangers in early specialisation before 13; some specialists, however, insist that guidance to take up a particular sport or event is necessary before 12 in order to ensure efficient skill development in the more complex technical events, like tennis, figure-skating, gymnastics and some track and field events.

The final point to make is that many tests would certainly appear relatively primitive to Western coaches. Most tests in the early selection stages are simple field tests, and the PE teacher's or coach's eye often provides the most ready information. Of course, the multi-stage process of testing, with potential talent being subjected to more sophisticated testing at later stages, undoubtedly improves the reliability of physical performance tests. While the reliability of initial testing is reckoned to be about 30% the reliability of the rate of progress during the first 18 months is said to be about 77%.

Sports schools

Once the young athlete is identified as possessing potential talent, he or she will be invited to join one of the various types of sports school. Here the budding athlete will enjoy certain privileges. Apart from expert guidance from trained coaches and regular examination and advice from sports medical specialists, he or she will enjoy completely free tuition and coaching, all costs being covered for training camps, and some educational privileges – for example, being given a longer period to complete educational courses or receiving an individually tailored course (as almost all student 'master' athletes do at the various institutes of physical culture).

Young people, then, who wish to pursue a sport seriously and to develop their talent may do so at one of the several types of school for gifted athletes (see Figure 5). At the base of the Soviet pyramid is the children's and young people's sports school (*detskoyunosheskaya sportivnaya shkola*) which young people can attend outside their normal school hours (they are, in fact, 'clubs' in the Western sense). The first

Figure 5 *Types of sports school in the USSR*

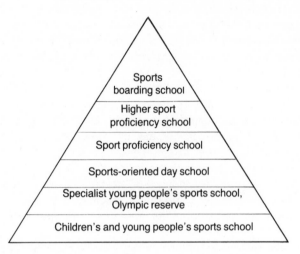

such school was said to be the Alexeyev School, opened in Leningrad in 1936.

Until 1981, these were entirely for children with some sort of promise or inclination for a particular sport. However, as part of the drive to involve more children in regular and active sports participation, a distinction was made in 1981 between such schools 'for all girls and boys irrespective of age and special talent for a particular sport' and those with the 'necessary amenities and qualified staff for training promising athletes'.[1] Henceforth, the former would be known as children's and young people's schools (CYPSS), while the latter would be called children's and young people's sports schools, Olympic reserve. The education authorities are responsible for financing and administering the former – roughly half the total number of the CYPSS, while the sports societies, especially Dinamo and the Central Army Sports Club, are responsible for the latter. Altogether there were some 8500 CYPSS with an enrolment of over 4,500,000 children in 1986.[2]

Children are normally considered for the CYPSS on the recommendation of their school PE teacher or at the request of their parents. Sports newspapers also carry items advertising entry trials to the schools. Attendance and coaching are free. While most take children at the age of 11, for some sports they may accept them earlier or later, depending on the parameters laid down by the USSR Sports Committee. In recent years, the age limits have gone down: since 1977, for example, the Moscow Dinamo CYPSS has had a gymnastics section for children between 4 and 6, the children attending three times a week – though training appeared (to the author) to be fairly general.

Each leading soccer and ice-hockey club (the major spectator sports are soccer in summer, ice hockey in winter) runs its own specialist 'nursery', providing a full course of training for promising young boys from the ages of 6 and 7 – these lower age parameters, too, have fallen from 9 and 10 in recent years.

Table 2 *Training programme of a Soviet gymnastics school* (1980)

Name of group	No. of groups	Age		No. of pupils in group	No. of sessions per week		Length of each session	
		Boys	Girls		Boys	Girls	Boys	Girls
Preparatory	3	9	8	15	2	2	2	2
'Young Gymnast'	3	10	9	15	3	3	2	2
3rd Rank	3	12	11	12	3	4	3	2
2nd Rank	2	13	12	8	4	3	3	3
1st Rank	2	15	13	6	4	4	4	3.5
Candidate Master of Sport	1	17	14	4	5	5	4	3.5
Master of Sport	1	18	15	3–4	5	5	4	3.5

Source: Tipovoye polozhenie o detsko-yunosheskoi sportivnoi shkole (DYUSSH),
(Moscow, 1980), p. 25.

The USSR Sports Committee lays down typical conditions of work for all the sports schools. The programme for special gymnastics schools gives some idea how serious the training and attendance are taken (see Table 2). Not all the schools in practice observe the statute. For example, during several study visits to gymnastics schools over the last decade, the author noted that in Minsk and Leningrad, 7-year-olds attended the gymnastics sections four times a week, arriving for each two-hour daily session at 9 a.m. (they attended normal secondary schools on the second shift in the afternoons). The 11-year-olds attended six days a week for three-hour sessions. The annual cycle of training consisted of preparatory work for the first three months of the year, followed by eight months of competitive gymnastics (10 internal and 22 external

competitions) and one month of transitional work. The weekly timetable
was as follows:

Monday – introductory work, comprising some 500 exercises;
Tuesday – heavy training;
Wednesday – heavy training;
Thursday – light training;
Friday – medium training;
Saturday – heavy training, followed by a sauna;
Sunday – day off.

Given that fairly rigorous schedule, it is perhaps hardly surprising that
the drop-out rate in Minsk was relatively high: of the initial intake of 330,
only a tenth survived two years later.

While initial testing of candidates was confined to height, weight, the
parents' (and grandparents') physical measurements, and the children's
gymnastics results, it later became more thorough as the gymnasts
underwent extensive tests at the city sports clinic. The tests covered
heart, blood, urine and muscle tissue. Besides access to the more
specialised sports clinic in the city, the Minsk school also had its own
medical treatment centre on the premises. While this is not always the
case with all such sports schools, they do seem to be well served with
both qualified (four-or five-year degree) coaches and sports doctors.

The principal aim of the sports school is to use the best of limited
resources to give special and intensive coaching to children in a
particular sport so that they may become proficient, gain a ranking and
graduate to a national or city team. An examination of the sports
pursued at the specialist sports schools leaves no doubt that the chief
targets are the Olympic sports. The sports practised most in the schools
are track and field, basketball, gymnastics, volleyball, swimming and
skiing.

The specialist schools are naturally provided with the best resources in
the country: of the 65,000 full-time coaches, over half were working in
the sports schools. Altogether, some 50,000 coaches and sports doctors
were operating in the schools in the mid-1980s. It is, moreover, the
prescribed duty of the country's full-time athletes to undertake regular
coaching and to give displays in the schools. Another advantage of the
schools is that they have access to facilities, particularly for technical
sports, that are generally in short supply. In 1982, for example, over 80
per cent of the country's figure-skaters and high-divers, most of the
swimmers, and a third of all gymnasts pursued their sports in these

schools.

Another type of school is the sport-oriented day school (*obshcheobrazovatelnaya shkola s sportivnym profilem*), which combines a normal school curriculum with sports training – on the model of the foreign-language-oriented schools. Then comes the sports proficiency (*shkola sportivnovo sovershenstvovaniya*) and the higher sports proficiency (*shkola vysshevo sportivnovo sovershenstvovaniya*) schools, which provide extra-curricular training for schoolchildren and students on short-term (usually three-month) vacation courses. The distinction between them is normally one of age – students between 16 and 18 attend the former, those 18 and over the latter.

At the apex of the pyramid are the sports boarding schools (*sportivnaya shkola-internat*). The USSR opened its first sports boarding school 'on an experimental basis' in the Central Asian city of Tashkent in 1962 – on the model of similar schools founded a few years earlier in the GDR. In East Germany, four such schools (*Kinder- und Jugendsportschule*) had come into existence in 1952 (in Berlin, Leipzig, Brandenburg and Halberstadt) following a government decree in 1951 – just two years after the GDR's foundation. By 1988, the GDR had 27 residential sports schools (involving 10,000 youngsters) – though half the Soviet total in that year, they amounted to ten times more in per capita terms. About the same time China had 300 'high level' sports schools with 30,000 junior athletes, many of whom were boarders.

It was only in 1970 that a special Soviet government resolution put the seal of approval on such schools in the USSR, by which time 20 existed, distributed about the Republics. By 1984, there were 40 sports boarding schools with an enrolment of 14,211 pupils – approximately 355 pupils per school. Each school practises an average of ten sports; all the sports are Olympic except chess (featured at one school, in Baku, home of the world chess champion, Garry Kasparov), although the Olympic sports of shooting and sailing are not included. The schools are run and financed jointly by the USSR Ministry of Education and the USSR Committee on Physical Culture and Sport (Sports Committee) attached to the USSR Council of Ministers. Local supervision is the joint responsibility of the Republican education ministries and sport committees.

They follow other specialised boarding schools (e.g. mathematical, musical, artistic) in adhering to the standard curriculum for ordinary secondary schools, but have an additional specialised study-load in sports theory and practice. Their aim is for pupils to obtain the school-leaving certificate in addition to proficiency in a particular sport.

Boarders are accepted from between 7 and 11 depending on the sport, and stay on until the age of 18 – a year longer than at ordinary secondary schools (to enable them to cover the academic curriculum). Room and board, as well as coaching fees and travel expenses to competitions, are paid for by the state. Boarders also have the advantage of a special nutritious diet: at the Tashkent school, it was reported that the daily food expenditure of the school per pupil amounted to 1 rouble 64 copecks, virtually double that (84 copecks) at ordinary boarding schools.

Boys and girls are normally invited to the schools on the basis of their performance in Republican school games, though some are attracted by advertisements placed in the sports press. Following the decision to expand such schools in 1981, a number of advertisements appeared in the daily newspaper *Sovetsky sport*. Thus, one advertised for:

> 13–15-year-old talented throwers: boys at least 185 cm, girls 175 cm. You are invited to come to Moscow for three-day trials. To take part you should let us know your name, date of birth, height, weight, sports results and your school record. Written permission from your parents is essential . . . Those who are successful will be invited to continue their studies in secondary sports-profile boarding schools of Olympic training centres, free of charge. The training will be under the supervision of senior coaches of the USSR throwing team.[3]

It is a measure of the need to attract sufficient candidates that this advertisement was made in the form of a letter from the country's leading throwers (Melnik, Chizhova, Lusis, Bondarchuk, Sedykh, Kula and Kiselyov).

Once at the school, allocation of periods to sport in the timetable rises with each successive year of the course. For example, at a sports boarding school the author visited in Tallin in 1981, 12-year-olds in the gymnastics section spent 25 hours per six-day week on standard school subjects, two on swimming, two on general physical education and eight hours on gymnastics. In the top form, at 18, they devoted 23 hours a week to sport, including 19 hours of gymnastics. Roughly the same number of hours had to be spent on academic work. Despite these rigorous schedules, it is frequently asserted that pupils at sports boarding schools have a better-than-average health and academic record: the physical and mental aspects apparently supplement and reinforce each other.

While some of the schools are well equipped, some have relatively poor or no sports facilities at all. The Tallin school commanded three gymnasiums, a 25 m indoor swimming pool, a ski centre, a track and field stadium with tartan track, and courts and fields for a variety of games. The Tashkent school grounds cover an area of 20 hectares and include a three-hall wing for gymnastics, indoor and outdoor swimming pools, and an indoor running track. On the other hand, the Leningrad sports boarding school that the author visited in 1980 had no sports facilities at all and had to rent them (though facilities were planned). Similarly, it was reported that the Frunze school, founded in 1968, had no sports amenities and its pupils had to train in a local sports club on even days and a physical culture institute on odd days, both being at the other end of the city. About the same time, children at the Pervomaisky District sports boarding school in Moscow had to travel to other parts of the city in order to use amenities like a swimming pool and indoor track and field stadium. Doubtless, such a situation will improve as sports construction catches up with boarding school creation.

The motive for establishing the sports boarding schools has been the conviction that giftedness in sport has to be developed at an early age if it is to have an opportunity to blossom to the full. This is especially so in such sports as track and field, swimming, gymnastics and figure-skating, where early specialisation would seem to be essential to the attainment of high standards and success in international competition. The three sports of track and field, gymnastics and swimming together account for nearly two-thirds of all medals at the summer Olympic Games.

It is no secret that the schools are expected to produce Olympic champions and that they have a political as well as an educational purpose:

> The sporting vocation has a practical importance not for mass sport, but for specialised sports schools in such disciplines as track and field, gymnastics, swimming, team games, figure-skating, skiing and speed-skating – i.e. in sports that constitute the basis of the Olympic programme. In assessing the significance of sport in international competition, we should remember that, while world and European championships are very important, victory at the Olympics acquires a political resonance.[4]

The point being made is that the Olympic Games carry more publicity and more national prestige. They are regarded by some as *the* measure of a nation's health and vitality. They are, further, the only visible sphere in which the USSR and other socialist states have overtaken the major capitalist powers.

It is thus regarded by many concerned with sports excellence as advantageous to bring children with an instinctive aptitude for sport into the 'controlled' environment of a residential school, where they are provided with the best coaches and amenities, nurtured on a special diet, supervised and tested regularly by medical staff, and stimulated by mutual interest and enthusiasm.

All the same, the schools are not without their critics: some object that they lack depth and cannot produce a sustained flow of world-class athletes: the only answer, they say, is to provide more facilities for the population at large. After all, the number of children attending these and other types of sports schools amounts only to just over 3% of all schoolchildren. Other detractors have decried the marked acceptance of privilege implicit in the very existence of the schools. The respected economist Professor Birman had a letter published prominently on the front page of *Sovetsky sport*, recalling Lenin's words that 'libraries should take pride in the number of readers they attract, not the rare books they have in their repositories'. 'Surely', Prof. Birman writes, 'Lenin's words apply equally to sport?'[5]

The schools are also accused of encouraging the formation of an elite based on the luck of nature's draw and thereby perpetuating original inequalities rather than properly compensating for the lottery of birth. Some educationists are concerned about the study-load imposed upon the children and the efficacy of combining mathematics and soccer, and the possibility of academic work being overshadowed. In a frank article in the weekly youth magazine *Sobesednik*, the former ice-hockey star Yevgeny Zimin writes that he must

> confess with shame how frivolously I treated my studies . . . apart from ice hockey I knew nothing and so could only count later on work in a sports organisation . . . Although athletes are a strong breed, they aren't able to defend themselves and are prey to those coaches and sports administrators who cultivate them in hot-house conditions so that they are unsuited to real life.[6]

The biggest stumbling block in the early stages of promoting sports boarding schools was parental opposition to giving up their children to the schools. One source admitted in 1971 that

> the sports boarding schools so far do not show the slightest popularity among parents – for various reasons. First, parents don't like the word *internat* [boarding school], perhaps because of its association with institutionalised care of the deprived. Then the word *sport* puts them off. They find it embarrassing to tell their neighbours that 'My Sasha is in a sports school'.
>
> One parent is quoted as telling her neighbour that her daughter was in a special 'physics' rather than 'physical culture' school.[7]

Largely because of such parental opposition, the Minsk boarding school was on the verge of closing down in 1971, and the situation was just as precarious in several others. The soccer boarding school (with some 100 pupils) in Voroshilovgrad, attached to the 1972 soccer champions club Zarya, had trouble in getting started, but not from parents. It met opposition from trainers at children's and young people's sports schools who were afraid of losing some of their charges.

In recent years, particularly encouraged by the new atmosphere of openness, the Soviet media have featured increasing criticism of elite sport and the privileges and 'distortions' resulting from the accent on sports excellence. A number of publications have drawn attention to the lack of sports facilities for the general public and the low level of participation in sport by young people. Others have focused attention on the unsavoury outcome of a 'win at all costs', 'running after medals' philosophy. In a blistering attack on a number of disgraced top athletes, coaches and sports administrators, the weekly magazine *Ogonyok* in early 1987 wrote that 'No medals can replace what is most valuable for us – a human being . . . No matter how pleasant the victory, it must never become an end in itself, a terrible need to do anything to attain it.' And the journal warned that 'sport reflects the realities of the world about it. And the Party-proclaimed regeneration process is powerfully making inroads into areas that only yesterday were forbidden-to-criticism zones.'[8]

The nature of such comments and the apparent effectiveness of parental opposition suggest a fairly low status for sport as a vocation, at least in the opinions of an important section of the public. While officials may see in the sports boarding schools a more efficient way of controlling the use of free time of young people and using it for sports training, many parents would seem to dislike the idea of greater state control over their children than is absolutely necessary through attendance at ordinary schools and the Pioneer youth organisation.

None the less, after a period of teething troubles the schools of sporting excellence, particularly the boarding schools, do seem to have gained considerable approval and justified themselves at least in terms of providing many of the top athletes in the USSR and the world. And trends in other countries, often inspired by the Soviet and other socialist state (GDR, Cuba, China) treatment of sports giftedness, seem to be towards the spread of sports boarding schools. Purists may well argue, with some justification, that this is yet another step in the race for irrational glory that should find no place in a socialist society. The practitioners, on the other hand, may consider it to be a natural development in a centrally planned state to concentrate resources to maximum effect in order to win victories in today's highly competitive, specialised world of sport.

By contrast with the USSR and most other economically developed socialist states, the provision for sporting excellence in the Western world differs considerably both between nations and between 'amateur' and 'professional' sports. Although there have been tentative efforts to start sports boarding schools (the USA and Canada had one each in 1989; Britain started up its first one, for soccer, in 1984; France and West Germany had six each), they cannot measure up in any serious way to the co-ordinated network of free sports schools in communist states.

Sports rankings exist in some Western states for a narrow range of sports (swimming, gymnastics, track and field), but screening, performance prediction, the application of science and medicine to sport, all vary considerably in effectiveness over sports and nations, and all suffer from lack of co-ordination (if not outright hostility) between coaches, athletes, sports officials and government. Status, work conditions, certification and effectiveness of coaches also differ so widely that no generalisation is possible. For example, the USA hired its first full-time national coach in track and field in 1982; Britain followed suit three years later; and Germany employed its first in 1913, and West Germany had 13 – plus another 11, one in each of its federal states – in 1988. While West German sports organisations began a coaching certification programme in 1974, it, like similar programmes elsewhere, is not compulsory. Effectively, anyone can become a coach in the West, while only fully trained men and women who have completed government-approved courses can coach full-time in communist states. Advantages accrue from both systems, although in terms of sporting achievements, especially at the Olympics, there is little doubt which of the two has proved more successful.

Notes

1 See *Sovetsky sport*, 24 September 1981, p. 1.
2 *Zhenshchiny v SSSR 1988. Statisticheskie materialy* (Finansy i statistika, Moscow, 1988), p. 32.
3 'Priglashenie k konkursu metatelei', *Sovetsky sport*, 18 February 1982, p. 4.
4 I. V. Prokorev, 'Olimpiada i politika', *Teoriya i praktika fizicheskoi kultury*, no. 5, 1968, p. 42.
5 Letter to *Sovetsky sport*, 18 October 1974, p. 1.

6 Quoted in Yuri Bychkov, 'Schastlivchik?', *Sobesednik*, no. 35, August 1986, p. 12.
7 See *Moskovskaya pravda*, 26 February 1971, p. 4.
8 Stanislav Tokarev, 'Ne proigrat by cheloveka', *Ogonyok*, no. 9, February 1987, p. 20.

Chapter Seven
Sports medicine

An examination of sports medicine cannot cover all the communist countries since their traditions and current conditions are all so disparate. Sports medicine in China, for example, owes much to traditional Chinese folk remedies which exist cheek by jowl with the latest computer-aided medical treatment. This chapter therefore concentrates attention on just two countries: the USSR and the GDR, both of which have been extremely successful in the world of sport and whose success has partly rested on their advanced sports medicine.

Sports medicine in these two countries is of particular interest for three principal reasons:

 (i) it is an area of communist sport the West knows little about;
 (ii) it is a vital and integral part of communist sport;
(iii) it is an area of sport that the West is most backward in.

In regard to (i), apart from the writings of ex-GDR athletes and medical specialists now living in the West (Mader, Kühnst, Vogel)[1] and some symposium papers, little is known of communist sports medicine. In any case, in English-speaking countries particularly, virtually no sports medical specialist has sufficient knowledge of an East European or Asian language to read specialist literature published there. Nor have the sports medical institutions (e.g. the Kreischa medical rehabilitation centre in the GDR) been readily accessible to Western visitors.

With more understanding and information, it would be less easy to fall back on stereotypes bred of ignorance – such as communist sports success being based on 'wonder drugs', hypnosis, or ethical malpractices.

As to (ii), we have already seen that the communist nations, first and foremost the USSR and GDR, came to dominate the Olympic Games and many other world and continental tournaments. The contribution of sports medicine to these sporting achievements is generally recognised in East and West as being significant.

The statement under (iii) clearly needs qualification. Several advanced Western nations possess excellent sports medical facilities. They also have first-class specialists – doctors, physiotherapists, exercise physiologists, psychologists – willing to give up time and money for the good of sport. They have researchers who lead the world in the treatment of sports injuries, in biomechanics, sports psychology, prognosis and diagnosis, and much besides. But none have a *system* of sports medicine. And all suffer from fundamental defects that militate against effective service to sport. None include sports medicine in their health services.

Increasingly, demands for more open and serious studies of communist sport and sports medicine are coming from Western coaches and athletes. To give but one example, in the build-up to the 1984 Olympics, US athletes expressed a desire for better information, medical expertise and equipment to enable them to compete successfully with athletes from the leading communist nations. Out of this need grew the Sports Medicine Committee and the Sports Equipment and Technology Committee of the US Olympic Committee. One of the first tasks of these co-ordinating committees was to conduct a survey during 1983 of the various national governing bodies and athletes' advisory council members in each of the 36 sports in summer and winter Games. The 36 sports were classified into three categories – high, medium and low – according to the level of technology and expertise (including medical) used. An important element of the survey was to establish how US Olympians fared by contrast with those of other countries, as well as how the athletes themselves perceived their comparative strengths. The results are expressed in Table 3. It is evident that the USA tends to do well only in those sports in the low technology and expertise category. Technological and sports medical superiority have been clearly concentrated within the USSR and GDR.

The irony is that the USA as a nation was far ahead of the USSR and GDR in overall technological progress; it was its planned application to sport that was lacking. The survey also discovered that US participants in the 36 sports obtained most of their technological and medical information from each other or from an informal network of coaches and other competitors rather than from a central 'data bank' and specialist periodicals (like the GDR's monthly *Medizin und Sport*) which the authorities make available to all.

Before proceeding to an examination of sports medicine in the USSR and GDR, two caveats ought to be made.

Table 3 *Number of sports in which a country is judged the technological leader*

Country	High-technology sports	Medium-technology sports	Low-technology sports	All sports
USSR	4	5	3	12
USA	0	3	8	11
GDR	6	0	2	8
West Germany	2	2	4	8
Japan	0	1	4	5
Canada	1	2	0	3
Eastern Europe (excluding USSR & GDR)	0	1	2	3
Italy	1	1	0	2
Holland	0	2	0	2
France	0	1	1	2
Others*	3	3	2	8

*Seven nations in all: Denmark, Finland and Switzerland had 1 high-technology sport each; Sweden, Spain and Norway had 1 medium-technology sport each; Great Britain had 1 low-technology sport

Source: Donald E. Schuele, 'Technological profile of Olympic sports', *Mechanical Engineering*, no. 97, 1984, p. 82.

First, of all the nations of Eastern Europe the GDR was the most economically advanced, though it lagged some way behind the economically advanced Western states in terms of GNP and general living standards. The USSR is the most developed of the world's under-developed states, and not vice versa. Sports treatment and equipment in both countries, therefore, are often unsophisticated and scarce by Western standards. It is the overall system (by contrast with the lack of it in the West) that produces the results: a determination actively to apply theory to practice; a system that plans its sports research programme far ahead; and a machinery which attempts to organise the best possible way of achieving its aims.

Second, sports medicine is an extremely wide concept that embraces far more than monitoring, diagnosis, treatment of injuries, and talent forecasting of top-class athletes. It includes industrial hygiene, mass physical fitness and the rehabilitation of general medical patients (especially those with cardiovascular and metabolic ailments) through sports therapy.

Brief history and definition of sports medicine

In Eastern Europe generally, disagreement existed for many years over what actually constituted sports medicine. Even today, although sports medicine has established itself as a full and independent discipline, its parameters are by no means fixed or universally accepted by either the sporting or the medical profession. The polemic is not merely academic: it reflects differences over emphasis (especially on sport for all or on sporting excellence), the status of sports medical experts and government commitment. Further, marked inter-state differences abound, often reflecting diverse traditions, development and priorities.

In the USSR, the government State Committee on Science and Technology employed the term 'sports medicine' (*sportivnaya meditsina*) in a special resolution for the first time only in 1977, thereby signalling official approval of sports medicine as an independent discipline. Hitherto the entire area spanning medicine and sport had, since 1918, been described largely as 'medical supervision' (*vrachebny kontrol*) of sport and physical recreation. We have to bear in mind that Soviet Russia had no sports science heritage to speak of and that in 1917 the Bolsheviks had taken over a semi-feudal, peasant and illiterate country that was in a state of war-ruin and chaos, a land with an inclement climate, where disease, epidemics and starvation were common, and where most people had only a rudimentary knowledge of hygiene. The country suffered from epidemics of social diseases such as syphilis, trachoma, scabies and other skin infections, even cholera, leprosy, tuberculosis and smallpox; the average life expectancy was 32 in the European part of the country.[2] It is in this context that the role of sports medicine must be viewed in the pre-war years 1917–41.

Arguments over the status of sports medicine are by no means resolved. Some Soviet specialists regard it as a science in its own right; others see it as what the eminent German specialist Ernst Jokl once described, in reference to Western sports medicine, as a mosaic of multifarious activities existing in isolation from one another. There can be no doubt, however, that since the government resolution of 1977 the pendulum has swung towards accepting sports medicine as a fully fledged scientific discipline.

In the GDR, on the other hand, sports medicine enjoyed official support as an independent discipline at least after 1953 when the Sports Medicine Committee (*Fachausschuss für Sportmedizin*) was attached to the Health Ministry. Unlike the USSR, the GDR was only created in 1949, inherited a scientific study of sport from before the war, had an economic and industrial infrastructure more advanced than that of the USSR, and was not concerned with a rapid transition of backward peasants to the town, with disease and deprivation, with a vast land and a multinational population. One immediate implication of this difference from the point of view of health and sport was that the GDR was not faced so urgently with the problem of using exercise and physical culture for developing physical and social health – it never adopted, for example, a system of 'production gymnastics' at places of work.

One overriding diplomatic problem facing the GDR after the war was to gain international acceptance of the country as an independent state. Hence the high priority that the authorities accorded to the development of sport and the GDR's international performance. One result, naturally, has been a big fillip to research (including and especially through sports medicine) into top-performance sport.

In the same year as the creation of the Sports Medicine Office, people of diverse medical specialisms interested in sports medicine came together to form a 'working group for sports medicine' in order to stimulate interest among general medical people in sports medicine; this group later became the GDR Sports Medical Society (*Gesellschaft für Sportmedizin der DDR*), whose founding members were Stanley Ernst Strauzenberg, two other general physicians, Arnold and Grimm, and an anatomist, Kurt Tittel. Tittel was the sports medical representative in a sports study group of 14 that went to the USSR in 1954 for six weeks. The purpose of the visit was mainly to study Soviet methods and take back Soviet experience. As a result, the Soviet sports medicine system (along with the sports system) was more or less transplanted to the GDR, with Soviet textbooks translated into German (like A. N. Krestovnikov's *Ocherki po fiziologii fizicheskikh uprazhneniy – Essays on the Physiology of Physical Exercises* – which appeared in the GDR as the country's first sports medicine textbook in 1953). Another product of the visit to the USSR was the 'importing' of a number of Soviet sports medical specialists to help get things moving. The most notable and influential was Professor Sergei Ivanov, who spent three years at the Deutsche Hochschule für Körperkultur (German Academy of Physical Culture) at Leipzig in the early 1960s. All this was despite the pre-war pioneering German work in sports medicine by such eminent physicians as Mallwitz, Bier, Sauerbruch, Kolb, Loewy, Herxheimer, Kohlrausch and Arnold himself.

Sports medical dispensaries, set up on the Soviet model, initially offered a six-week crash course in sports medicine; they also encouraged research and gradually evolved into the first sports medical centres, located in all the major cities (Leipzig, Berlin, Dresden, Erfurt, Rostock, Halle, and Karl-Marx-Stadt, which is now Chemnitz once more). Their main task was quite unambiguously to work with and for top sports performers, to advise coaches on planning training loads, and to define the relationships between general and specialist training and between sex and age differences.

Initially, the medical profession was reluctant to accept sports medicine as a bona fide branch of medicine, especially as it seemed more geared to producing faster and stronger athletes and treating sports injuries than preserving the communty's health. But the government's priority in developing talented athletes to be standard-bearers for the GDR ultimately prevailed, and by the early 1960s the focus of sports medicine was very definitely on discovering talent, planning individual training regimes and treating sports injuries. In fact, centres of sports excellence (sports boarding schools) had been set up in 1951, so researchers had a ready-made laboratory for tests and experiments; it was also the job of medical specialists to advise on selection of children for the special sports schools.

In 1961 the sports medical monthly magazine *Medizin und Sport* began publication; apart from the *Hungarian Review of Sports Medicine* (which publishes material from all over the socialist world), it remains the only such specialist sports medical journal in Eastern Europe. In the same year two important sports medical institutions came into existence: the Sports Medical Institute attached to the Leipzig Academy, and the Sports Medical Rehabilitation Centre (later called the Central Institute of the Sports Medical Service) at Kreischa near Dresden. The latter was initially intended to study and improve the treatment and rehabilitation of injured and sick athletes, to accelerate their return to training and competition. That remained its main function as the GDR's major sports clinic. However, in so far as a general clinic for internal diseases is also attached to the Kreischa centre, it has led to the forging of an important link between sport and general health: experience gained from the treatment and rehabilitation of athletes has been widely applied to treating patients suffering from cardiovascular and metabolism disorders. This interaction between elite sport and routine clinical practice was particularly important since it helped to convince more of the doubters, especially in the medical profession, of the viability of sports medicine and its potential for improving public health.

By 1963 sports medicine was firmly enough entrenched for the government to set up the Sports Medical Service, responsible for all sports medical care throughout the country. As a result, all 15 regions (*Bezirk*) of the country soon had their own sports medical centres, while the 240 districts (*Kreis*) gained a small sports medical service headed by a qualified sports doctor.

In the relatively short span of its history, sports medicine in the GDR not only achieved full recognition as an independent discipline within the country; it made a vital contribution to advancing the GDR to the forefront of the world and earned the recognition of many countries as being the foremost centre of sports medicine in the world. It advanced from borrowed experience and foreign specialists to a fully independent sports medical service providing assistance to many other nations, including the USSR.

The GDR Sports Medical Association set out its official definition of sports medicine in the early 1960s: 'Sports medicine is concerned with the study of the human organism's reaction to sports activities and, on that basis, with promoting physical capacity and athletic performance.'[3] The main aim of sports medicine, by contrast with that of clinical medicine, was said to be to enhance the physical capacity of healthy, sick and disabled people of all ages. This early guide to development in the GDR was in line with international definitions and reflected both the relatively healthy condition of the population (by contrast with that of the USSR whose vital statistics – average life expectancy, morbidity, infantile mortality – are generally inferior to those in the GDR) and the early commitment to elite sport (in view of the rivalry between the two Germanys and the lack of diplomatic recognition of the GDR).

Sports medical practice and research, therefore, have been intended to encompass physiology, morphology and functional problems as well as pathophysiology, therapy and rehabilitation – not as a sum total of disparate elements, but integrated in the specific task of improving health and performance through sport. A sports medical specialist should thus be conversant with exercise physiology, functional anatomy and kinesiology; be capable of diagnosing and treating orthopedic and traumatological lesions or injuries as well as internal diseases; be aware of the need for and the possibilities of specialist diagnostic procedures and therapeutic measures, and of the typical effects of sports activities and training on an athlete's organism.

Such a specialism goes beyond the professional parameters of ordinary orthopedic and surgical doctors, of physiologists and specialists in internal diseases engaged in the sports medical care of athletes in the West.

The role of sports medicine

As might be expected in centrally planned societies, sports medicine is run by the state to deal with needs and priorities at a particular time. There is no commercial or private sports medicine; there is no individual fitness or health structure independent of that of the state-directed and funded service. As a Soviet specialist attests, 'sports medicine in the USSR, like medicine generally, is administered by the state, it is free, accessible to all and served by qualified personnel'.[4] Within the centrally planned sports system, sports medicine has its defined place and functions. These may be summarised as follows.

General medical examination of people engaging in sport.

This falls into three categories: initial, follow-up and supplementary. During the initial examination the doctor's task is to decide whether a person should pursue a particular sport or not. Without a medical certificate no coach, recreation officer, or teacher of physical education may admit any newcomer to sports activity or physical education at school or club.

The medical check-up is concerned with the overall state of health, physical development, and ability to cope with physical loads. In the follow-up test the doctor checks on the effect of regular sport and exercise on the person's state of health, physical maturity and functional condition. Such tests are compulsory no less than once a year for all people registered at clubs and sports centres.

Supplementary medical check-ups take place when considering admission to competition and resumption of training after illness or injury, after lengthy gaps in playing, or if overstrain is apparent. Certain sports (boxing, marathon running and swimming, walking and running over 20 km, skiing races of 50 km or more, long-distance cycling, motor-cycling and car racing, and underwater swimming) possess competition rules that make medical examination obligatory immediately before an event. Furthermore, all contestants in boxing and wrestling have to undergo a medical examination prior to weighing in for the bout.

'Dispensarisation' of full-time athletes

All proficient athletes must by law attend a dispensary once or twice a year for a thorough medical examination involving general clinical tests and examination of the athletes' physical work capacity and fitness for sports activity. The test is intended to ascertain the athletes' overall state of health and functional potential, to establish whether they have realised their potential, whether there are early signs of overstrain or overtraining, and to reveal pre-pathological conditions and deviations in health whose timely treatment would improve the physical state and work capacity.

Medical–educational supervision

This is an important component of the entire process of medical supervision of the health of people engaging in sport. It is undertaken jointly by the doctor and coach during instruction and training. The doctor has to observe the conduct of training sessions and changes in the athlete's functional state and training condition. Information obtained is considered when planning training schedules and determining the intensity of training loads.

Sanitary, medical and prophylactic action during training and competition

This work is carried out jointly by sports doctors and medical specialists from medical–prophylactic and sanitary–epidemiological institutions. Their responsibility is to ensure that conditions are clean, that no one is likely to pass on disease, and that all precautions have been taken to preclude infection and injury. In addition, it is the responsibility of the sports medical service to see that all sports equipment, clothing, footwear and defensive guards are in a safe and sanitary state. Day-to-day inspection is the task of the district sanitary and epidemiological offices in collaboration with sports doctors. Further, the state sanitary inspection office has to be consulted, along with sports doctors, when sports amenities are being designed and built.

Medical provision for sports competitions

Medical facilities have to be provided for all official sports competitions. In the absence of a medical official, the competition organiser has no right to commence or hold the event. Rules on types of obligatory medical service are laid down and depend on the size and level of each competition. Part of this service is intended to reduce the risk of injury.

Once a sports injury does occur it is treated either by the sports doctor *in situ* or at the local sports injury clinic. An additional branch of the service at large-scale events today is concerned with doping control.

Medical provision for mass sport
There has to be medical supervision of training and the taking of tests for the GTO national fitness programme, of 'production gymnastics' in the USSR, and of sport and recreation for middle-aged and older people in keep-fit groups. It is the responsibility of the sports medical 'cabinets' to supervise the preparation for and taking of GTO tests. Medical and sanitary provision for 'production gymnastics' falls on the sports medical dispensaries and cabinets responsible for this work jointly with officials of the prophylactic establishment.

Health education work among athletes
This is intended to instil hygienic habits into athletes in regard to their everyday lives, work, studies and training. A major task of the sports doctor is to teach the athlete independent supervision, regularly to keep a diary of self-supervision, to abide by the norms of personal and public hygiene, and to know how to administer first aid to himself.

Research and methodological work
Research into medical aspects of sport is an integral part of sports medicine. It is conducted in many higher educational establishments (including all the institutes of physical culture and the physical education faculties at universities and institutes), at medical colleges, the USSR Academy of Medical Sciences (and, most important of all, at one of its institutes: the Research Institute of Physiology and Physical Culture), and at the two physical culture research institutes in Moscow and Leningrad. Unlike many Western universities, Soviet and GDR institutions did not present a *carte blanche* to their postgraduate students in selecting themes for research. Nor do the institutions themselves have complete freedom of choice. Research is an integrated effort in which a department, college, region, or Republic receives an assignment from a higher body such as the Health Ministry or Sports Committee; all the institutions involved then pool resources to work on that assignment.

The Soviet Federation of Sports Medicine, headed in 1986 by Prof. Zoya Mironova, is responsible for disseminating research findings, convening meetings to discuss new directions in research, and maintaining contact with foreign colleagues through FIMS (the Fédération de Médecine du Sport). Research into sports medicine has a long history in the USSR. As long ago as 1934 a medical supervision laboratory was attached to the Central Institute of Physical Culture (then called the Stalin Institute). In 1972 it became the Department of Sports Medical Problems attached to the All-Union Research Institute of Physical Culture, which had taken over the former site of the Central Physical Culture Institute, now housed in new premises on the edge of the city of Moscow (at 4 Sirenevy Boulevard). Since 1980, in connection with the Moscow Olympics of that year, the Department of Sports Medicine has had its own five-storey building on the research site (Yelizavetinsky pereulok No. 10) with floors allotted to biochemistry, a neurohumoral laboratory, sports psychology, doping control and mass sport.

Organisational structure of sports medicine

The organisational structure of Soviet sports medicine is shown diagramatically in Figure 6, illustrating the chain of command from the USSR Health Ministry, associated with, though taking precedence over, the Sports Committee, down through the Soviet administrative divisions: Republic, region, city and individual sports stadiums, swimming pools, sports halls and sports schools. Overall planning and guidance lie with the Academy of Medical Sciences and the research institutes attached to the USSR Ministry of Health, while everyday work is in the hands of the various sports medical establishments: the dispensaries, cabinets, polyclinics, hospitals and health departments.

Like the GDR sports medical service, the Soviet system has two linked but separately existing components: for the community at large and for proficient athletes.

Sports medicine for the community

All people taking part in sport, including those undergoing their GTO tests, do so under the supervision of sports groups or clubs that have their own medical specialists working in so-called *sports medical cabinets*. It is the responsibility of the cabinets to examine all would-be and actual sports practitioners. Such cabinets, estimated at 10,000 in 1984 (served by 6500 sports doctors and 12,000 intermediate medical personnel), exist in all the major sports societies (Spartak, Dinamo, Army), sports centres (stadiums, sports halls, pools and tracks), educational institutions (schools, colleges and universities) and polytechnics.[5] Many of the

Figure 6 *Organisational structure of Soviet sports medicine.*

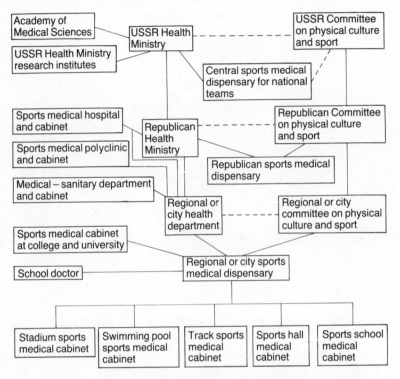

Source: V. L. Karpman, *Sportivnaya meditsina* (Moscow, 1980), p. 17.

larger factories, like Moscow's Likhachov Motor Works, also have their own polyclinics to which sports medical cabinets are attached. Funding is provided partly by the local health department and partly by the parent body: sports society, factory, or local education authority. Irrespective of their departmental affiliation, however, all sports medical cabinets come under the organisational supervision of the sports medical dispensaries.

Each person examined at the cabinets has a medical card (Form 227, known as the athlete's 'Medical Supervision Card'), and has to undergo tests of the following:

personal medical and sports history;
physical development (anthropometry): height, weight, strength;

Figure 7 *Organisation of the GDR Sports Medical Service.*

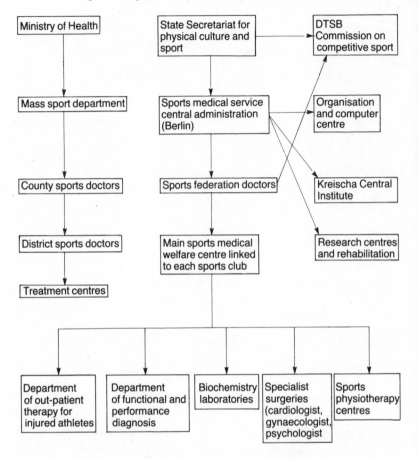

Source: W. Hollmann and A. Mader, 'Sportmedizin in der DDR', *Sportwissenschaft*, June 1983, p. 160.

nervous and cardiovascular systems;
respiratory organs;
digestive system;
excretion (urine and faeces).

Functional tests usually based on a few minutes of squats and jogging are additionally carried out for pulse, blood pressure, and the body's reaction to effort. Such an examination has to take place at least once a year for *all* people regularly engaged in sport and physical recreation. Additionally, any members of the public can avail themselves of the clinic's services free of charge for a general check-up with a view to sports participation. Saturdays are normally set aside for this open-door service to the public.

Sports medicine for athletes

All proficient athletes are attached to a *sports medical dispensary*. Such 'proficient athletes' include both promising young people in the various sports schools and those 'who are members of teams of Republics, regions and cities'. In other words, the dispensaries are for all more or less full-time athletes. Altogether there are over 450 Soviet sports dispensaries serving some 3 million athletes, including more than 1 million in Soviet national squads – that is, roughly one dispensary for 7,500 athletes or one for 2,500 national team members.[6] They employ some 5,500 sports doctors – that is, roughly 14 doctors for each dispensary.[7]

Funding for the dispensaries comes from the USSR Health Ministry or the appropriate local health department. The service is free, although costs are reckoned to run into 30 roubles for a general check-up and up to 600 roubles for a detailed examination.

The sports medical dispensaries do more than serve top athletes. Their responsibility is also

> to supervise, analyse, plan and take account of all the work done by the sports medical cabinets; they are remedial and prophylactic institutions with their own polyclinics, hospitals and research laboratories equipped with the latest technology and using modern methods of investigation, diagnosis and treatment as applied to the needs of sports medicine.[8]

They therefore act as a link between the officially stated twin aims of Soviet sport: *masterstvo* (proficiency) and *massovost* (sport for all).

While athletes in *city* teams would naturally be served by the *city* sports medical dispensary, *regional* teams by the *regional* dispensary, and *Republican* team athletes by the *Republican* dispensary, members of Soviet national teams have their own sports medical dispensary at the Lenin Stadium in Moscow (Podyezd No. 8) which has close ties with the All-Union Physical Culture Research Institute, the Laboratory of Sports Cardiology of the Central State Institute of Physical Culture, and several medical faculties at institutes of physical culture. Each national sports squad has a team of medical specialists from the dispensary assigned to it, constituting what is known as a 'comprehensive scientific group' that provides medical and biological expertise. The group works together with coaches to supervise and guide the work of the squad. Most of these medical specialists are experts in one particular sport or group of sports (e.g. soccer and rugby, Olympic gymnastics and modern rhythmic gymnastics, wrestling and judo). As well as national teams having their own doctors, every top league team (in, say ice hockey, soccer, basketball, volleyball) also has its own sports doctor.

All athletes attending a sports dispensary must undergo a thorough examination at least once a year, as well as four or five check-ups during the year. Particular attention is paid to pathologies in each sport. For instance, in so far as skiers take heavy loads on their legs and blood vessels, they are regularly examined by proctologists and urologists. Boxers and track cyclists, who are particularly prone to head injury, have regular extensive neurological check-ups ('brain scans').

National squad members must have a full examination twice a year and as many check-ups as is deemed necessary. Conventionally, the sporting year is divided into three periods:

preparatory / basic / competitive

The full medical examinations take place in the first two-thirds – that is, in the preparatory and basic phases – thereby ensuring that athletes are fully fit for the competitive season. At the end of the season, further-more, athletes are examined once again to decide on their immediate future: for example, at sanatorium, rest home, spa or hospital. Each athlete has a file (Form 227a, known as the 'Dispensary Observation Journal') on which the results of all tests are recorded.

For check-ups, the athlete sees no more than one or two doctors, but for the yearly or twice-yearly thorough examination, it is compulsory to be checked by the following:
sports medical doctor;
surgeon;
specialists in: sports injuries,
eye, ear and nose,
mouth (including teeth),
lungs,
biochemical analysis,
skin;
neuropathologist;
gynaecologist (women);

cardiologist;
urologist;
functional diagnostician.

The athlete must also undergo functional tests before, during and after exercise. Once all the specialists have been seen and the results are known, the athlete is treated, where necessary, by the appropriate specialist. Dispensaries must have their own sports injuries departments complete with physiotherapy and rehabilitative facilities (pool, hydromassage, sauna) and a small hospital for longer treatment of sports-specific injuries. Any athlete who has to be hospitalised for specialist treatment is likely to be sent to the central sports hospital in Moscow. Originally a special sports wing of the Central Railway Hospital, since the late 1970s it has had its own hospital building and separate facilities.

In recent years it has also become increasingly the responsibility of sports doctors at the dispensaries to establish training loads. As Lev Markov, chief physician at Moscow's No. 1 Sports Dispensary puts it,

> Examinations are no longer enough. The sports doctor is becoming an assistant to the coach in determining loads, in structuring the training process, and in selecting suitable athletes for training. In recent years a number of dispensaries – for example, in Moscow, Sverdlovsk and Vilnius – have gained new well-equipped laboratories for assessing and forecasting the functional state of athletes.[9]

Markov's Moscow Dispensary has 9000 registered athletes served by 100 doctors and 200 auxiliary medical personnel.

Not all sports doctors are happy about the rising pressure on the medical profession to supervise and sanction the enormous training loads, especially on young children. Professor Zoya Mironova, recipient of the International Olympic Order and the Philip Noel-Baker medal for services to sport, has written that 'With the colossal loads that are today placed on the immature organism, the question of children's sports injuries assumes paramount importance'.[10] What particularly worried her, following a visit to the Leninsk-Kuznetsky gymnastics school run by Igor Mamentyev, was that, although the 'school's success cannot fail to strike the imagination, the success would be even more imposing if it were not for one thing: at the most vital moment, when a first-class gymnast is being trained, the spinal column in some children suddenly begins to "give way" and they are beset by pain and injury'.[11] On investigation, in fact, it was not the loads that were so much to blame as the lack of strict medical examination during the selection of gymnasts for training. Owing to parental pressure to get their daughters into the school, and the eagerness of coaches to accept them, the local doctors had succumbed to the pressure and neglected such problems as curvature of the spine. It was only when a substantial load was put on the child's organism that the weakest link would 'snap'. As Mironova attests, 'One has only to reduce the loads and the physical traumas disappear. But it is much more difficult to cure the psychological injuries when a gymnast has to give up sport through injury.'[12]

The specialist medical service described above is also extended to athletes from certain other socialist nations (e.g. Cuba) and from some developing countries of Africa, Asia and Latin America.

Professional training in sports medicine

The issue of the professional status – and hence training – of sports medical specialists has been sensitive in both the USSR and the GDR. The concern, naturally, is that sports doctors might 'fall between two stools', between medicine and sport, earning the respect and recognition of neither. They should therefore be skilled in the treatment of disease and other disorders, as well as opting for a medical discipline like surgery or neuropathology. After all, 'athletes fall ill with normal diseases unconnected with sport, as well as with diseases caused directly by sport or, rather, by irrational training methods'.[13]

So sports medicine ought to be concerned with clinical medicine. A sports doctor should therefore be able to diagnose and advise on the training process, yet be able to treat ordinary patients as well. As Strauzenberg has written.

> There are only a few physicians engaged in traditional medical areas who are able to contribute to preserving health on a sound scientific basis. The student of medicine and, in most cases, the physician in a medical discipline, is trained to diagnose and treat disease. If there is no symptom, the doctor often sees no reason for treatment. The sports medical specialist, on the other hand, is experienced in examining and evaluating the functional capacity of the organism, and knows that there are differences in states of health – i.e. states that cannot be taken as 'morbid' even though they restrict capacity. This restriction can often presage a manifest disease or pave the way for pathological processes. It can and must be treated, not primarily by prescribing drugs but by active measures to restore lost capacity. That implies, naturally, a thorough knowledge of the amount and type of training and exercise appropriate to individual circumstances, based upon an expert judgement of the functional state of the patient.[14]

In Strauzenberg's opinion, sports doctors have to be informed on physical capacity and performance as well as on appropriate treatment for reduced capacity. They are invaluable to the coach and the athlete and, equally, to physicians in other clinical fields who are interested in curing diseases and restoring their patients to full capacity. They should not only serve sport, they should serve medicine as well, and contribute to helping athletes attain their potential and to improving the health and well-being of the community. 'We are fully convinced that good physical capacity is one of the most important conditions of a happy and meaningful life . . . A major objective of the sports physician, therefore, is to help as many people as possible to attain and maintain physical fitness.'[15]

All the same, there are some specialists who fear that the emphasis has shifted over the last 20 years from mainly examining athletes and treating injuries to maximising performance. 'Modern sport entails greater physical and emotional loads on young bodies, and the role of sports medicine increases proportionally with their growth.'[16] Perhaps that is why GDR sports officials latterly put so much emphasis on the sports doctor being 'a specialist in matters of physical stress and performance as well as in treating deficiencies in stress and performance. He is seen as the indispensable partner of the athlete and the coach.'[17]

In terms of professional training, there was no disagreement in either country that a sports medical specialist must take a *full medical degree*. The following two options exist:
(1) A medical degree in a seven-year course (six years of theory and clinical practice, plus one year's practical work in one's chosen specialism) followed by a special sports medicine course – varying in duration from six months to two years. The sports medical course normally includes sports therapy, functional diagnosis, physiotherapy, traumatology, biochemistry and pharmacology, plus a specialism. The course may be taken at most medical institutes.
(2) A physical culture course followed by a full medical degree course. Since some athletes and others with a physical culture background wish to become sports doctors at the end of their active sports career, they have the opporunity to take a part-time degree in physical culture (as either teacher or coach) while still active in sport, and then devote themselves to medicine. This method does not require a special sports medicine course following the medical degree since a physical culture diploma course contains elements of sports medicine. All the courses contain two years of biochemistry and sports

biochemistry; two years of medical supervision and sports pathology; one year each of human anatomy, physiotherapy, sports morphology, psychology and sports psychology, hygiene and sports hygiene, and biomechanics; and, for women, three years of remedial physical education (men do military training).

Two final points ought to be made here, distinguishing the GDR system from most Western sports systems.

First, all full-time coaches in the USSR and GDR *had to* have a coaching certificate in a 'sports' course in physical culture (four years full-time, five to six years part-time). They are consequently skilled specialists in their own sport, with a detailed knowledge of a scientific discipline and sports medicine.

Second, the typical career pattern of a Soviet or GDR athlete was to take a degree course in physical culture on a part-time basis and have an individually tailored degree course lasting five or more years. On retirement from active sport, the athlete will have a qualification and a profession to take up, often within the sports movement as coach, recreation officer, sports official, or PE teacher; or he or she can study to become a sports doctor. It is possible for full-time athletes to register as students of medicine during their active sports career, but the intensive study and clinical work involved in the degree make this difficult. None the less, some athletes have done so. For example, in 1984 the Olympic champion sprinter Marita Koch was taking a medical degree at the Wilhelm Pieck University in Rostock; the gymnast Karen Janz was just completing her medical qualifications in the third year of medical practice at Berlin's Charité Hospital; the former Olympic swimming champion Kornelia Ender was in her third year of medical studies at the Friedrich Schiller University of Jena, while her ex-husband, the former swimming champion Roland Matthes, was a dental student in Erfurt. Barbara Kische (née Wieck), 800 m world champion in 1965, had completed her medical studies in Rostock, worked in a local sports injuries clinic for three years as her compulsory post-degree practice and was, in 1984, working as medical specialist in track and field in the region. As one last example, the European high-jump champion of the early 1960s, Gerd Dührkop, had taken a physical culture course during his active career, then studied medicine in Rostock; on graduation he worked two years in university clinics as assistant, gaining experience; went to the Leipzig DHFK for three months, working with Tittel and Strauzenberg; transferred to Kreischa for clinical practice to complete his qualifications; and subsequently became a sports medical doctor in charge of the sports medical centre at Wismar.

Medical studies are intensive and standards are evidently not lowered for former athletes. After all, as sports medical professor at Jena University, Dr Joachim Scheibe, explained on failing gold-medalist Helmut Recknagel (he subsequently switched to veterinary surgery!), 'You cannot tell a grieving mother that "Sorry, your child has died through the doctor's negligence, though he does have an Olympic gold medal" '.[18]

Although the Soviet Union offers a full sports medicine degree at the Department of Sports Medicine at Tartu University in Estonia and the GDR was, in 1988 considering setting up a similar course at the Friedrich Schiller University under Dr Scheibe, the reluctance of the GDR to follow the Soviet example in establishing an independent sports medical department would seem to indicate that there was still a commitment to enabling the medical profession to retain its hold on the discipline and to ensuring that sports doctors were first and foremost medical practitioners with an interest in community medicine as well as in sports talent.

What price is society prepared to pay for talent?

With the unfolding of glasnost (openness) in a number of communist (and erstwhile communist) countries, a lively discussion has developed in the mass media on the price that society is prepared to pay for sports success. Not only has the debate centred on the relationship between the funding of top- and bottom-level sport, but also on the detrimental effects on people's health of their commitment to sports training.

The dark side of training and sporting victories is now coming increasingly under the spotlight. While it is admitted that 'young athletes have absolutely no legal rights', surveys have revealed that 'more than 35 per cent of young athletes have serious health problems. A major reason is overwork and unjustifiably heavy training schedules. Coaches try to produce champions as quickly as possible, and the result is chronic physical overexertion.'[19] One of the most dangerous sports (as it is everywhere in the world) is women's gymnastics. Leonid Arkayev, Head of Gymnastics of the USSR Sports Committee, was reported in the weekly *Ogonyok* – though he warned that it was *not* for publication – as asserting that 'there was not a single world-class gymnast performing today who had not been seriously injured'.[20]

The most poignant case of serious injury to a gymnast is that of Yelena

Mukhina, who broke her neck in training just prior to the 1980 Moscow Olympics. She has since been confined to a wheelchair, paralysed from the neck down. After breaking her leg in 1979, a year after becoming world champion, she even trained in a cast 'encouraged by her coach and not discouraged by the doctors'. The journalist commentating on this incident makes a damning indictment of Soviet sport – and indirectly of sports medicine:

> Why is it that victories are so important to us that we push athletes to the limit of their physical capabilities, apparently without concern for the risk? It is because we believe that sports success brings prestige to the country. What is more, we see success as proof of the correctness of the political path we have chosen; it is a symbol of our superiority. Hence the demand for victory at any price. As for the risk, well, what's a human life in comparison to the country's prestige? That's what we've had drummed into us since childhood.[21]

If concern for the health of athletes has been obscured for political purposes, it casts a shadow over the role of sports medicine, or at least that part of it that has worked on producing ever faster, stronger, more skilful athletes – at any cost. The area of greatest moral opprobrium has been that of performance-enhancing drugs. When a number of émigré athletes, coaches and sports doctors had previously talked of the widespread use of drugs in Eastern Europe, their testimony bore a suspicion of 'selling out'. Even when fairly recently, in 1989, the one-time East German ski-jump champion and later sports doctor, Hans-Georg Aschenbach, sold his story alleging that GDR athletes were drugged from childhood, he was widely attacked in East and West for sensationalism. Yet the substance of what he said was never successfully undermined. In fact, evidence has been emerging from the USSR since 1986 of just such state-controlled administering of drugs in the USSR and East Germany.

Back in 1986, Yuri Vlasov, then Chairman of the USSR Weight-lifting Federation (and subsequently outspoken radical in the first Soviet Parliament – the Congress of People's Deputies), declared that immense damage had been done to Soviet sport in general, and weight-lifting in particular, by the 'coach pharmacologist' who worked alongside the sports coach. Not only did Vlasov accuse Soviet athletes of using anabolic steroids 'for several decades', but he named names – specifically that of senior coach and Sports Committee official Arkady Vorobyov, 'who was one of the first to distribute anabolic steroids to members of our national team'.[22] A TV report made in late 1989 further revealed a document signed in 1982 by two deputy sports ministers, prescribing anabolic steroids as part of the preparation for Soviet cross-country skiers. The document set out a programme to test the effects of steroids and for research into ways of avoiding detection.[23]

It has long been known by those familiar with communist sport that drug-taking was organised *at the top* and involved parts of the sports medical establishment; no athlete was allowed overseas unless he or she had a clearance test at a sports medicine dispensary before departing. At the Olympics of Montreal (1976) and Seoul (1988), it has now been revealed, the Soviet team had a hospitality ship used as medical centre to ensure that Soviet competitors were 'clean' at the last moment.[24] Soviet coach Sergei Vaichekovsky, who had had overall charge of Soviet swimming from 1973 to 1982, had admitted that the use of drugs in Soviet swimming was widespread: 'From 1974 all Soviet swimmers were using banned substances . . . I've personally administered the drugs and advised swimmers individually on how to avoid getting caught.'[25] He indicated that while the East German method was to give drugs only during periods of intensive training, at the start of the year, Soviet swimmers took them to within a month of major meetings.

The USSR, like other countries, has long had a drug-testing programme centred on the 'doping control' laboratory in Moscow, which has been dealing with 'about 5000 analyses per annum at a cost of some $200 each'.[26] Until 1990, however, the results were never publicised. It was in that year, after much public criticism and international pressure, that the Sports Committee admitted that of the 4,077 tests made in 1987, 47 were positive; and in the three years prior to the 1988 Olympics, as many as 290 athletes and coaches had been punished. No sports or specific athletes were named.[27] A writer in the medical journal *Meditsinskaya gazeta* commented:

> Previously we knew very little about the drug testing system because all the results were kept secret. After the tests, a coded list with the names of those who tested positive was sent to the Deputy Chairman of the Sports Committee who determined punishment on an individual basis and never publicised the guilty parties . . . So sports officials could forgive whomever they wanted and, of course, had no interest in banning the stars.[28]

Since early 1990, however, because of public pressure the Sports Committee has promised that it will publish the names of athletes who fail the test; they will be banned for two years for a first offence and for life for a second offence; and coaches who encourage drug abuse are to be banned for life. It may be that in conditions of perestroika and glasnost, the nations of Eastern Europe will be able to use their undoubtedly advanced system of sports medicine for combating drug abuse in sport, averting exploitation of children for the sake of fleeting glory, and ensuring that, as one eminent sports doctor, Dembo, has put it, 'sporting achievements grow as a result of, not at the expense of, better health'.[29] It remains to be seen whether this will be so.

Notes

1 See Alois Mader, 'Verwissenschaftlichung des Sports in der DDR – sportmedizinische Erkenntnisse und ihre Anwendung', unpublished manuscript (Cologne, 1977); A Mader and W. Hollmann, 'Sportmedizin in der DDR', Sportwissenschaft, no. 2, June 1983, pp. 152–62.
Peter Kühnst, Des missbrauchte Sport. Die politische Instrumentalisierung des Sports in der SBZ und DDR 1945–1957 (Verlag Wissenschaft und Politik, Cologne, 1982).
Renate Heinrich-Vogel, 'Mein Lebensweg vom sportbegeisterten Kind zur Hochleistungssportlerin der DDR', in Dieter Ehrich, Renate Heinrich-Vogel and Gerhard Winkler, Die DDR Breiten- und Spitzensport (Kopernikus Verlag, Munich, 1981), pp. 49–59.
2 Nikolai Semashko, 'Desyatiletie sovetskoi meditsiny i fizicheskaya kultura', Teoriya i praktika fizicheskoi kultury, no. 5, 1928, p. 3.
3 Stanley Strauzenberg, 'Sports medicine in the German Democratic Republic', Medisport, no. 3, August 1981, p. 243.
4 A. G. Dembo, Aktualnye problemy sovremyonnoi sportivnoi meditsiny (Meditsina, Moscow, 1980), p. 9.
5 A. G. Safonov, Meditsinskaya sluzhba (Fizkultura i sport, Moscow, 1984), pp. 7–9.
6 V. D. Karpman (ed.), Sportivnaya meditsina (Meditsina, Moscow, 1980), p. 18.
7 Lev Markov, 'The doors are open for all', Sport in the USSR, no. 5, 1985, p. 39.
8 Karpman, p. 17.
9 Markov, p. 40.
10 Zoya Mironova, Forvard prodolzhayet borbu (Fizkultura i sport, Moscow, 1979), p. 354.
11 Ibid., p. 399.
12 Ibid., p. 400.
13 Dembo, p. 22.
14 Strauzenberg, p. 246.
15 Ibid.
16 Oleg Belakovsky, 'Doctor Belakovsky's stadium', Sport in the USSR, no. 11, 1984, pp. 26–7.
17 Mader and Hollmann, p. 157.
18 Personal communication from Dr Joachim Scheibe, Friedrich Schiller University, Jena, September 1983.
19 S. Dadygin, 'Smotrite v glaza molodykh', Pravda, 17 April 1989, p. 4.
20 Oksana Polonskaya, 'Vzroslye igry', Ogonyok, no. 29, July 1988, p. 12.
21 Ibid.
22 Yuri Vlasov, 'Drugs and cruelty', Moscow News, no. 37, 1988, p. 15.

23 Reported in *Sovetsky sport*, 10 October 1989, p. 1.
24 Vasily Gromyko, 'Nash styd', *Leninskoye znamya*, 28 March 1989, p. 2.
25 Reported in *Corriere Dello Sport*. See Alan Page, 'Sacked Soviet official admits widespread use of drugs', *Guardian*, 2 December 1989, p. 20.
26 Yelena Kokurina, 'Kto shutit s chortom . . .', *Meditsinskaya gazeta*, 4 January 1989, p. 4.
27 *Ibid.*
28 *Ibid.*
29 Dembo, p. 24.

Chapter Eight
Sport and foreign policy

Ever since the first communist state came into existence in 1917, communist leaders have made explicit the dependence of external sports relations on foreign policy. It could hardly be otherwise in countries where sport is centrally directed and employed in the pursuit of specific socio-political objectives, including those of foreign policy. We have already seen that sport is a political institution run by the state, and that overall sports policy is laid down by the government. Decisions of national import concerning foreign sports policy – such as participation in the Olympic Games or in particular states disliked by the government – are therefore made by the ruling party and government. On occasion it is a supranational body, like the Warsaw Pact, rather than a sovereign government, that decides policy, as in the case of the Soviet-led boycott of the Los Angeles Olympics in 1984. And for those communist states in Eastern Europe that have been closely bound to the USSR, it has often been the Soviet Politburo that has imposed a 'fraternal' sports policy upon them.

That is not to say that all communist leaderships act in collusion. China and Romania participated in Los Angeles in the face of Soviet opposition. Cuba and Ethiopia acted in solidarity with North Korea in boycotting the Seoul 1988 Olympics, while all other communist states (save Albania which has boycotted all Olympic Games) competed. It is likely that concerted communist efforts will continue to be dissipated in the 1990s. Indeed, although communist external sports relations have in the past kept pace with the evolution and sometimes zigzag course of communist foreign policy, there are signs that, as communist sport becomes more and more involved in commercial contracts and East–West agreements, and as individual states take a more independent line, future government-dictated sports policy itself is likely to play less of a role than it did in the past. The following statement has become both an embarrassment and a subject of derision throughout Eastern Europe:

The mounting impact of socialist sport on the world sports movement is one of the best and most comprehensible ways of explaining to people all over the world the advantages that socialism has over capitalism.[1]

External functions of communist sport

The role of sport in communist foreign policy has varied in importance over the years, reflecting both shifts in domestic and foreign policies and the rapidly changing world situation. In the years from 1917 to 1948–49, when the USSR either constituted the sole communist state in the world or held undivided sway over the communist movement, it was Soviet policy that dictated communist involvement in world sport. But following the Soviet break with Yugoslavia in 1948 and the communist revolution in China in 1949, the Soviet monopoly was broken.

On the whole, however, five major aims seem to have been pursued in communist sporting relations with the rest of the world – some more or less consistently and others only in one or another phase of foreign politics or involving a particular group of communist states. We can consider the pursuit of these state goals as functions assigned to the sports movement and attempt to assess how successfully it has coped with discharging them.

Promoting relations with pro-communist and potentially sympathetic groupings abroad and undermining 'bourgeois' and social-democratic authority

The scope of communist foreign sports contacts has depended on a number of factors, not all of them controllable by the communist leadership. This has been notably so when not only 'bourgeois' but also other communist (e.g. Chinese, Albanian, Romanian and Yugoslav in defiance of the USSR) governments and sports organisations have refused to play.

After the 1917 Revolution, when Soviet Russia's territory was seen as a salient and *place d'armes* on the front of the class war and the expectations of world revolution dominated its foreign policy, the tendency was to boycott 'bourgeois' sports federations and the Olympics, and to promote sports contacts with worker sports organisations rather than with governments. Since the international labour movement, and its sports organisations were, however, split into social-democratic and communist factions, Soviet sports ties were mainly confined to 'sympathetic' foreign worker clubs. Some attempts were made, none the less, in the

'United Front' and 'Popular Front' periods (1927–37) to use sport to bridge the gap between the two rival factions – without marked success.

After the Second World War, with the new balance of power in the world, particularly after the emergence of several new communist states (including China in 1949) and the vigorous launching by the USSR and its allies of the 'peaceful coexistence' policy in 1953, and with the desire by several communist states to measure their strength against the best world opposition, the accent on competing against worker teams has diminished, though it has not completely disappeared. Examples of the pursuit of such goals since the war are of two main types.

First, there is the promotion of sports contacts with labour organisations abroad, such as those with the Finnish Labour Sports Union (TUL), the French Workers Sport and Gymnastics Federation (FSGT) and the Austrian Workers Sport and Cultural Association, and participation of communist athletes in a variety of worker tournaments, such as the annual running and cycling races through Paris and Moscow (sponsored by the French communist newspaper l'Humanité and the Soviet government daily Izvestiya respectively). They include, too, the annual Peace cycling race across Eastern Europe and the World Youth Festival, in whose programme sport plays a central part.

Second, sports contacts exist with trade and professional associations, such as those with the International Sports Union of Railway Workers and the International Federation of University Sport. In regard to the latter, international university games had been held at two-yearly intervals since 1923, but without communist participation up to 1946. In 1946 there was formed a new International Union of Students (IUS) whose sports section that year arranged student games in Paris in which Soviet students made their international debut. However, the domination of the IUS and its sports section by the student unions of communist states and their sympathisers in Western student unions led to the student games of 1949 and 1951 being given an explicitly political slant by being combined with communist-sponsored World Youth Festivals. A split occurred when several Western student unions tried to prevent their members taking part in the youth festivals and set up in 1949 a breakaway organisation – the International Federation of University Sport (FISU). Between 1949 and 1958, the two student sport organisations held their games separately; they came together again in 1959 when all the student sport organisations of Eastern Europe (except those of East Germany and Albania) were admitted, on application, to FISU. As mutual compromises, the sports council of the IUS was dissolved and the FISU Games were renamed Universiad or World Student Games. The communist states continue to hold their youth games within the bounds of the overtly political World Youth Festival, although prime attention is today concentrated on the Universiad.

Since 1945, there has been no serious effort to turn either communist or social-democratic sports organisations into alternatives to the existing sports federations, as had happened prior to the war. Nor has 'loyalty' to communist sports federations (like the French FSGT) been permitted to interfere with sports relations with non-communist states. The new situation was brought about by a number of factors.

First, the Soviet Union had broken its isolation. It had emerged from the war a victor, its military and political power having penetrated into Central and Eastern Europe. As we shall see below, in the circumstances of international friction, or Cold War, which developed, with two rival blocs confronting one another in a divided Europe, sport became an arena for international competition, for 'defeating' one's ideological opponent. In the USSR, domestic sport was now thought strong enough to take on the world and victories over bourgeois states would evidently demonstrate the vitality of communism. During the war, the Red Sport International had gone the way of the Comintern, being dissolved in 1943, and henceforth, especially once the communist states had joined the IOC in the early 1950s, most ruling communist parties lost interest in a distinctly different worker sports movement.

Second, with the process of decolonisation and steady democratisation of both the Olympic movement and bourgeois sport generally (with fewer and fewer sports and clubs being confined to middle-class white males), the belief grew that international sport, particularly the Olympic Games, could be used for peace, international understanding and the isolation of racist regimes like that of South Africa.

Despite these changes in policy, the communist–social-democratic mutual suspicions and wrangling within worker sport survived the pre-war period, and the social-democratic International Workers Sport Committee was a fervent supporter of US-led efforts to boycott the Moscow Olympics of 1980.

Promoting neighbourly relations with geographically close states for strategic reasons and for demonstrating the progress made by kindred peoples under communism

One relatively stable element in sport's role as a diplomatic and propagandist medium has been to promote relations with geo-graphically close states and with newly-independent or dependent nations in Africa and Asia and, later, Latin America. This is particularly evident in relations between Cuba and the countries of South America, between China and the rest of Asia, between East and West Germany, and between the Soviet Union and its immediate neighbours.

The USSR and China, it has to be remembered, border on a dozen or more states and have a history littered with feuds and bloody clashes with neighbouring peoples. Both the Iron Curtain and the Great Wall of China are testimony to the attempts to keep out intruders.

For the Soviet Union, the neighbours in Europe are Norway, Finland, Poland, Czechoslovakia, Hungary and Romania; immediate neighbours in Asia are Turkey, Iran, Afghanistan, Mongolia, China and North Korea. Countries whose geopolitical situation brings them within the category of strategically important 'neighbours' of the USSR are evi-dently Sweden and Denmark in the Baltic area, Bulgaria, Albania and Yugoslavia in the Balkans, Austria in Central Europe, Japan (and now, after the Seoul 1988 Olympics, South Korea) in the Far East, and several countries in the Middle East.

In the 1917–45 period, when the USSR was the sole communist state in the world, contacts with developing states were naturally limited by the hold that the imperial powers still had over Africa, Asia and Latin America. In any case, the USSR's ability to bargain with the Great Powers was severely restricted by its weakness and isolation as well as by the mistrust in which it was generally held. On the other hand, the USSR was less handicapped in dealings with its immediate neighbours, all of whom were relatively weak and vulnerable; some, like Turkey and Persia, saw it as vital for their survival and independence to pursue neighbourly relations with the USSR as insurance against Soviet encroachment and as a warning to other Big Powers not to trespass into Soviet border areas.

The overall Soviet objective from the outset in regard to the country's neighbours and those states within strategically important areas close to the USSR was, as the historian Max Beloff has written, 'to link these [states] to Russia by treaties embodying the three major principles of "non-intervention", "non-aggression" and "neutrality" '.[2]

In pursuance of these principles, right after the Revolution, Soviet Russia signed a series of treaties with neighbouring states: Estonia, Lithuania, Latvia and Finland in 1920, Poland, Persia, Afghanistan and Mongolia in 1921. It was hoped by Soviet leaders that these treaties might render the neighbours less likely to serve as bases for a renewed imperialist crusade (following the failed intervention by Britain, France, Japan and the USA in Russia in 1918–21).

In regard to the imperial colonies of Africa and Asia, it has to be further borne in mind, that as the revolutionary fires faded in Europe (in Germany and Hungary) in 1918, Soviet leaders began to turn their attention eastwards, seeing the East rather than the West as the centre of the revolutionary stage, and the national liberation movement in those states (headed mainly by the national bourgeoisie) as a bulwark against Western colonialism. As the first Soviet Foreign Minister, Leon Trotsky, put it,

> The road to India may prove at the given moment to be more readily passable and shorter for us than the road to Soviet Hungary. The sort of army which, at the moment, can be of no great significance in the European scales can upset the unstable balance of Asian relationships, of colonial dependence, give a direct push to an uprising on the part of the oppressed masses, and assure the triumph of such a rising in Asia.[3]

Soviet and later overall, especially Chinese, communist policy was, therefore, to provide every assistance to national liberation movements in the colonies and newly independent states, including those on their frontiers, even where this conflicted with the interests of indigenous communists. China is the celebrated case in point: millions of communists were slaughtered by Chiang Kai-shek's Kuomintang forces which the USSR had backed. It is essential to an understanding of Soviet relations with the rest of the world, including in sport, from the early 1920s to bear in mind, therefore, that Soviet leaders were concerned *less with the export of revolution than with the strengthening of the USSR as a nation-state*; they argued that a wider proletarian revolution could only take place *after* the fortifying of socialism in Soviet Russia. As Stalin made clear,

> The very development of world revolution . . . will be more rapid and more thorough, the more socialism is reinforced in the first victorious country, the faster this country is transformed into a base for the further unfolding of world revolution, into an instrument for the further disintegration of imperialism.[4]

In terms of practical policy, therefore, Stalin sought alliances with 'bourgeois' and even 'feudal' states that were close to the USSR.

Sports contacts reflected these diplomatic and strategic considerations. Indeed, sport, being evidently 'apolitical', was seen as one of the most suitable vehicles for cultural diplomacy. As a Soviet sports leader was later to write,

Sport effectively helps to break down national barriers, create international associations, and strengthen the international sports movement. It is an immense social force helping to establish and promote international contacts between national sports associations of countries with different political systems.[5]

There was yet another role assigned to Soviet (and later Chinese) sport from the 1920s up to the present. Regional contacts with bordering states, especially in the Asiatic part of the USSR, were used for demonstrating the advances made by kindred peoples under socialism. It has to be remembered that in 1922, of the 140 million Soviet citizens, some 30 million, mainly Asiatic peoples (Turkic by language, Islamic by culture and Muslim by religion) still pursued a semi-feudal, pastoral, or tribal form of life, similar to that followed by kindred ethnic groups across the border in Turkey, Persia, Afghanistan, Mongolia and China. At this time, cultural, economic and health levels were analogous on both sides of the divide. From the outset, Soviet policy was for the relatively economically advanced parts of the USSR to help bring about a major social change in Soviet Central Asia (the Republics of Turkmenia, Uzbekistan, Kirghizia, Tadjikistan and Kazakhstan). The epoch introduced by the five-year plans (from 1928 onwards) brought rapid economic and social development – official indices of industrial production show a 12-fold increase in these regions between 1926 and 1940.[6] Revolutions similarly occurred in literacy and vital health statistics. Contacts between kindred peoples on either side of the Soviet border increasingly demonstrated, therefore, the great strides forward being made by Soviet peoples under socialism.

Contacts with states on the southern and south-eastern border – Afghanistan, Mongolia, China and North Korea – developed only in the mid-1950s. Sports agreements with Afghanistan were concluded from 1955 and exchanges have taken place regularly between Uzbek and Afghan athletes, particularly since the entry of Soviet troops into Afghanistan in 1979. It was reported in 1981, for example, that Soviet Tadjik wrestlers were training Afghan wrestlers at Kabul University.

Exchanges with Mongolia and North Korea commenced in the mid-1960s when those two nations were preparing for entry into the Olympic Games; both adopted the Soviet sports structure, including army and Dinamo dominant clubs.

With China, sports relations have closely followed the course of the Sino-Soviet dispute. Bilateral contacts, which began only in 1955, were abruptly halted in 1961. After the Cultural Revolution, resumption of political contacts between China and the West, which was said to have been presaged by table tennis matches in 1971 (the so-called 'ping-pong diplomacy'), was not paralleled by a similar renewal of sports contacts with the USSR. That had to wait until the 1980s when tentative efforts were made, following world championships in the two countries, to improve sports relations. For example, after the World Gymnastics Championships of the autumn of 1981 in Moscow, Chinese gymnasts remained in the USSR for a week 'at the invitation of the USSR Sports Committee', training in the Central Army Sports Club and giving displays round the country.[7]

All the same, it was not until 1986 that the first bilateral sports exchange agreement was signed in Beijing between the respective sports committee chairmen; it provided for the exchange of 40 sports groups, involving 550 athletes and coaches over three years. A new co-operation protocol was signed in Moscow the following spring, providing for joint competitions and training sessions in 12 sports. As the Chinese Deputy Sports Committee Chairman, He Zhangleang put it, 'Soviet–Chinese ties, restored after some 20 years, are now developing dynamically.'[8]

Winning support for communist states and their policies among developing states in Africa, Asia and Latin America

Since the break-up of colonial empires, particularly since the enthusiastic reinforcement of the 'peaceful coexistence' policy by the USSR and its allies in the early 1960s, with its concomitant East–West contest for influence over the development and politics of the 'Third World', the communist authorities have paid increasing attention to aid to developing countries in sport as well as in the economic and cultural spheres. This sports assistance takes the form of sending coaches and instructors abroad, building sports amenities, training foreign sports administrators, arranging tours and displays by communist athletes, and holding sports friendship weeks that often have an unabashedly political character. Much of this aid, including the provision of sports facilities and travel (e.g. to the 1980 Moscow Olympics) is said to be given free of charge. Sometimes the sports contact is used as a prelude to political contacts. After all, 'Sporting ties are one way of establishing contacts between states even when diplomatic relations are absent.'[9]

The most widespread form of assistance is for coaches to work abroad in developing states. By the 1980s, for example, Soviet coaches were working with national teams in over 30 developing states.

Another form of sports assistance to developing countries is the free provision of training and coaching courses in the communist states. As many as 44 developing countries of Africa, Asia and Latin America are said to have sent coaches and officials to study at the Moscow Physical Culture Institute by the early 1980s. So great was the demand that special short-term courses had to be set up from 1980 at the Moscow Institute with instruction in English, French and Spanish. Similar courses were set up in the GDR, Cuba and China.

Other forms of assistance in sport include the building of sports centres and provision of free equipment. Further, in preparation for national championships and regional games, a number of national teams use communist sports camps and sports medical centres: for example, Algerian judokas, Guinean swimmers, Tunisian volleyball players, Angolan track and field athletes and wrestlers, Kuwaiti swimmers, Yemeni track and field athletes, Afghan wrestlers, boxers and basketball players used Soviet amenities in the 1980s. Help is also given by specialists in arranging sports festivals – as, for example, the Central African Games held in Angola and the Asian Games held in India.

Judging by the rapidly mounting scale of operations for promoting sport in developing nations, the communist leaders evidently regard sport as an important weapon in the 'battle for people's minds'. It is a serious business: 'the authority of sport in the world has grown considerably; there is no longer any place for dilettantism in the politics of sport'.[10] Given the signal success of the communist states in the Olympic Games, such sporting aid is seen as an effective means of demonstrating the possibilities of the 'socialist path of development'. It is admitted that the USSR spends as much as 2.5 million roubles annually on the 'sports aid programme to Africa, Asia and Latin America – more than any other country'.[11]

In arranging contacts and assistance, much emphasis is placed on the propaganda value of the successes attained in the erstwhile backward areas of the USSR:

> In establishing these contacts, we attach special importance to the sports organisations of the various republics, to athletes from Kazakhstan, Uzbekistan, Azerbaijan, Armenia and Georgia, when they visit Africa and Asia, and when the representatives of those countries meet our Republican athletes at home.[12]

Not all sports 'politicking' has had favourable results. Following the decision of the Marcos regime in the Philippines to take part in the

Moscow Olympics (with travel and accommodation paid by the USSR), a high-level Soviet sports delegation went to the Philippines. During their meeting with President Marcos, the President said,

> we can learn much from our Soviet friends, including in sport. In many areas the Soviet Union has far outstripped all other states . . . I want you to convey to the Soviet government that the Philippines wishes to be friends with the USSR and to live in peace. My best regards to President Brezhnev, I wish him long happy years and good health.[13]

Neither Marcos, nor Brezhnev were to enjoy those last sentiments, and the opportunism on the part of the Soviet authorities was to rebound upon them in the years to follow.

One final aspect of Soviet 'aid' to developing countries has been support for Third World campaigns against racial discrimination in sport. The Soviet Olympic Committee instigated moves in 1962 within the IOC to exclude South Africa from the Olympic Games; the moves succeeded and South Africa has subsequently not been able to compete in the Olympics. The communist states have also lent their considerable authority to moves to have South Africa banned from all international sports tournaments. Today, it is only Western nations and athletes that continue sporting contacts with the apartheid regime in such sports as motor-racing, golf, boxing, horse-racing, tennis and rugby.

There would seem little doubt that many in the Third World see the communist states, first and foremost the USSR, as the major champions of their cause in the world sporting arenas and forums.

Maintaining and reinforcing the unity of the socialist community and the Soviet 'vanguard' position within it

In so far as sport is centrally controlled in all communist states, it can be wielded for manifestly functional purposes. After all, 'sports contacts help to strengthen fraternal co-operation and friendship and develop a sense of patriotism and internationalism among young people of the socialist states'.[14] From the Soviet point of view, this has enabled Soviet leaders to employ sport to try to integrate the various socialist societies, to bind them to Soviet institutions and policies and to maintain and reinforce the USSR's 'vanguard' position within the community. Relations have tended to reflect the political tenor within the group, with the USSR having defended (or imposed) its 'special relationship' as the 'first socialist state', and the other socialist nations having striven for compensatory supremacies denied them elsewhere. In the period 1948 to 1956, most of the other socialist states (with Yugoslavia the notable exception) were more or less obliged to learn from the Soviet model, to form Soviet-type administrative structures, to make army and security forces (Dinamo) clubs dominant, and to run fitness programmes like the Soviet 'Prepared for Work and Defence' – this despite the long sporting traditions of Hungary, Czechoslovakia and Germany, all of which had competed successfully in international sport many years before Soviet participation. Since 1956, however, there has been a gradual loosening of the Soviet grip on sport in other socialist states. Albania has gone its own way, initially following China, while other states have resurrected certain national sporting traditions and institutions which were submerged during the late Stalin era. Thus, the Sokol gymnastics movement played a major part after 1989, once more, in Czechoslovak sport, and East Germany pioneered the use of sports boarding schools in the early 1950s. In place of Soviet-dictated exchanges, new bilateral agreements have been drawn up and negotiated separately between the USSR and other socialist states.

Sports contacts between the socialist states embrace a variety of sports and take place at various levels. Athletes from these countries have come together in such single-sport tournaments as the annual Peace cycle race across Eastern Europe, the Znamensky Brothers Memorial Track and Field Meet in Moscow, and the '26 Baku Commissars Memorial' track and field tournament held in Baku; and in such multi-sport meetings for specific groups and organisations as the Friendship sports journeys for junior athletes, socialist rural games, twinned city games, the Baltic Sea Week and annual sports meetings between army and security forces sports clubs.

The sporting ties between the army and security forces clubs are particularly illustrative of the Soviet policy of military integration – or, at least, they put a friendly face on some of the possibly less popular aspects of the Warsaw Pact. A Sports Committee of Friendly Armies (SCFA) was formed in Moscow in 1958, three years after the establishment of the Warsaw Pact. It embraced all members of the Pact together with China, North Korea and North Vietnam. Neither the Pact nor the SCFA included Yugoslavia. Cuba joined the SCFA in 1969; China, Albania and North Vietnam took no part after 1960. The declared aims of the SCFA have been 'to strengthen friendship between the armies, improve the quality of physical fitness and sport among servicemen and to popularise the attainments of army sport'.[15] Each year, up to 1990, the SCFA arranged, on average, 15 army and Dinamo championships in a variety of Olympic and paramilitary sports, including special spartakiads in summer and winter.

The sporting aid given by the USSR and other countries with communist governments to Cuba was part of the process whereby that country was drawn into the ambit of the system of state socialist powers after a period of isolation and hesitation. The immediate aim was to help harness and build up Cuban skill in order that Cuba might put up a good showing in sporting confrontations with other American states. In the years 1969–72, 'more than 50 Soviet coaches helped train Cuban athletes for the Olympic and Pan-American Games'.[16] The subsequent Cuban successes in both tournaments provided ample material for linking sports success with the political system and demonstrating through the popular and readily understandable (particularly so in Latin America) medium of sport the advantages of the 'Cuban road to socialism' for other Latin American states. Fidel Castro was later to talk of Cuban Olympic success as 'a sporting, psychological, patriotic and revolutionary victory'.[17]

During the 1970s and 1980s, a number of coaches and instructors from socialist states, including Cuba, came to assist Soviet athletes in sports in which the Soviet standard was below world class. As a number of countries in the socialist community built up specialised facilities and expertise, they became increasingly able to help other athletes within the bloc to gather together on the eve of important international events for joint training (e.g. before the Olympics). These and other forms of mutual assistance and integration are said to have become an important contributory factor in the sports successes of such states internationally. They also demonstrate how seriously the leaders of these states have regarded sport as an eminently efficacious means of advertising the advantages of socialism and demonstrating the superiority of their system. *Pravda* has written of how 'the grand victories of the USSR and the fraternal countries vividly demonstrate that socialism opens up the greatest opportunities for physical and spiritual perfection'.[18] It has to be remembered, none the less, that special high-level arrangements have to be made for such sports co-operation within the community, inasmuch as free movement of citizens among these countries has not been part of their mutual treaty arrangements.

Attaining sporting supremacy, particularly through the Olympic Games, principally for the purposes of gaining recognition and prestige for communist states and for communism generally

Where other channels have been closed, success in sport would seem to have helped such countries as the USSR, China, Cuba and the GDR as well as many other states of the developing world to attain a measure of recognition and prestige internationally, both at home and abroad. The German Democratic Republic is perhaps the prime example. Boycotted for so long by the West and its athletes refused visas by NATO states to travel to international tournaments, it quite demonstrably poured funds into sport to establish itself as a world power to be recognised and reckoned with. As Party Chairman Erich Honecker made clear,

> Our state is respected in the world because of the excellent performance of our top athletes, but also because we devote enormous attention to physical culture in an endeavour to make it part of the everyday lives of each and every citizen.[19]

Sport here is unique in that for virtually all modernising societies, including the USSR and China, it is the *only* medium in which they have been able to take on and beat the economically advanced nations. For the socialist states this takes on added importance in view of what their leaders have traditionally seen as the battle of the two ideologies for influence over the world:

> the mounting impact of socialist sport on the world sports movement is one of the best and most comprehensible means of explaining to people all over the world the advantages that socialism has over capitalism.[20]

Cuba's leader, Fidel Castro, looks forward to the day when Cuba can prove the superiority of its national sport, baseball, over that of US baseball:

> One day, when the Yankees accept peaceful coexistence with our country, we shall beat them at baseball too and then the advantages of revolutionary over capitalist sport will be demonstrated.[21]

And a leading Soviet sports official makes the point that,

> The increasing number of successes achieved by Soviet athletes . . . is a victory for the Soviet form of society and the socialist sports system; it provides irrefutable proof of the superiority of socialist culture over the moribund culture of capitalist states.[22]

Despite some setbacks there is ample evidence to show that the economically advanced socialist states have gone a long way to achieving their aim of world sporting supremacy, especially in the

Olympic Games, as Table 4 shows. They have provided two of the top three nations in the summer Olympics since 1968 (save 1984 when they provided two of the top four despite overwhelming communist boycott of the Games) and in the winter Games since 1972.

Table 4 *Medals won by the top six Olympic teams, 1952–88*

Year and venues of Olympic Games	National Olympic teams	Medals			National Olympic teams	Medals		
		Gold	*Silver*	*Bronze*		*Gold*	*Silver*	*Bronze*
		Summer Olympics				Winter Olympics		
1	2	3	4	5	6	7	8	9
1952	USSR	22	30	19	Norway	7	3	6
	USA	40	19	17	USA	4	6	1
Helsinki	Hungary	16	10	16	Finland	3	4	2
	Sweden	12	13	10	Austria	2	4	2
Oslo	West Germany	0	7	17	West Germany	3	2	2
	Finland	6	3	13	Sweden	0	0	4
1956	USSR	37	29	32	USSR	7	3	6
	USA	32	25	17	Austria	4	3	4
Melbourne	Austria	13	8	14	Finland	3	3	1
	Germany	6	13	7	Sweden	2	4	4
Cortina	Hungary	9	10	7	USA	2	3	2
d'Ampezzo	Great Britain	6	7	11	Switzerland	3	2	1
1960	USSR	43	29	31	USSR	7	5	9
	USA	34	21	16	USA	3	4	3
Rome	Germany	12	19	11	Sweden	3	2	2
	Italy	13	10	13	Germany	4	3	1
Squaw	Hungary	6	8	7	Finland	2	3	3
Valley	Poland	4	6	11	Norway	3	3	0
1964	USSR	30	31	35	USSR	11	8	6
	USA	36	26	28	Norway	3	6	6
Tokyo	Germany	10	22	18	Austria	4	5	3
	Japan	16	5	8	Germany	3	2	3
Innsbruck	Italy	10	10	7	Finland	3	4	3
	Hungary	10	7	5	Sweden	3	3	1
1968	USA	45	28	34	Norway	6	6	2
	USSR	29	32	30	USSR	5	5	3
Mexico City	GDR	9	9	7	Austria	3	4	4
	Hungary	10	10	12	Sweden	3	2	3
Grenoble	Japan	11	7	7	France	4	3	2
	West Germany	5	10	10	Holland	3	3	3

Table 4 *Medals won by the top six Olympic teams, 1952–88 – (continued)*

Year and venues of Olympic Games		Summer Olympics				Winter Olympics			
	National Olympic teams	Medals			National Olympic teams	Medals			
		Gold	*Silver*	*Bronze*		*Gold*	*Silver*	*Bronze*
1	2	3	4	5	6	7	8	9
1972	USSR	50	27	22	USSR	8	5	3
	USA	33	31	30	GDR	4	3	7
Munich	GDR	20	23	23	Norway	2	5	5
	West Germany	13	11	16	Holland	4	3	2
Sapporo	Hungary	6	13	16	Switzerland	4	3	3
	Japan	13	8	8	West Germany	3	1	1
1976	USSR	49	41	35	USSR	13	6	8
	GDR	40	25	25	GDR	7	5	7
Montreal	USA	34	35	25	USA	3	3	4
	West Germany	10	12	17	West Germany	2	5	3
Innsbruck	Poland	7	6	13	Austria	2	2	2
	Romania	4	9	14	Finland	2	4	1
1980	USSR	80	69	46	GDR	9	7	7
	GDR	47	37	42	USSR	10	6	6
Moscow	Bulgaria	8	16	17	USA	6	4	2
	Poland	3	14	15	Norway	1	3	6
Lake	Hungary	7	10	15	Austria	3	3	2
Placid	Romania	6	6	13	Finland	1	5	3
1984	USA	83	61	31	GDR	9	9	6
Los Angeles	Romania	20	16	17	USSR	6	10	9
	West Germany	17	19	23	USA	4	4	0
	China	15	8	9	Finland	4	3	6
Sarajevo	Italy	14	6	12	Sweden	4	2	2
	Canada	10	18	16	Norway	3	2	4
1988	USSR	55	31	46	USSR	11	9	9
Seoul	GDR	37	35	30	GDR	9	10	6
	USA	36	31	27	Switzerland	5	5	5
	South Korea	12	10	11	Finland	4	1	2
Calgary	West Germany	11	14	15	Sweden	4	0	2
	Hungary	11	6	6	Austria	3	5	2

Before the Second World War, apart from sports exchanges between the USSR and Nazi Germany in 1940, few official representatives of foreign states had visited the Soviet Union for a sports event, nor had Soviet athletes competed, save on rare occasions, with athletes other than those belonging to worker sports associations. Nor had Soviet sports federations joined or been invited to join international federations. Further, since tsarist Russia's participation in the 1912 Olympic Games, no Russian or Soviet team had contested the Olympics.

With the expansion of communist states to 13 by 1949 and in the mood of patriotic fervour immediately following the war, it was felt that communist sport was strong enough to take on the West and, in the words of a Soviet Party resolution on sport, 'win world supremacy in the major sports in the immediate future'.[23]

In the main, communist states made their Olympic debut at the 15th Summer Olympics, staged in Helsinki in 1952. In view of the lack of previous experience against world-class opposition, their performance was remarkable, especially that of the USSR and Hungary. As Table 4 shows, Hungary took third place in the medal table (taking 16 gold medals to West Germany's none). Although the USSR gained fewer gold medals than the USA (22 : 40), it gained more silver (30 : 19) and bronze (19 : 17) and tied with the USA in points allotted for the first six places (according to the system used in the *Olympic Bulletin*). The political significance of this first West v. East confrontation had been apparent in the call by the IOC President Avery Brundage prior to the Games: 'Since for the first time these Games will provide a direct comparison between our boys and girls and those from the communist world, it is essential that we send our best and strongest team.'[24] Sports and political leaders on both sides of the Iron Curtain were well aware from the outset of the importance of the Olympic rivalry between capitalist and communist sport.

The communist countries took no part in the 1952 Winter Olympics and made their debut only in 1956 at Cortina d'Ampezzo in Italy. There, the 'vanguard' nation of the communist world, the USSR, amassed more medals and points than any other competing nation, winning gold medals in ice hockey (which it had only taken up after 1945), skiing and speed-skating. There was no mistaking the boost that Olympic success gave to the pride of the Soviet leadership – and people – in their athletes. Nor were Soviet political leaders slow to appreciate the benefit the USSR and other communist states could derive from their enhanced reputation at home and abroad. By a decree of the USSR Supreme Soviet of 27 April 1957 (after the USSR, in the 1956 Melbourne Games, had gained more medals and points than any other nation in Olympic history), a large group of Soviet athletes, coaches and sports officials were rewarded with some of the country's highest honours. The surprisingly high number of 27 beneficiaries received the supreme honour of the Order of Lenin.

And so it has continued. The USSR has gone on to dominate the Olympic Games, summer and winter, challenged only by the German Democratic Republic which gained more medals than the USA in the 1976 and 1988 summer Games, and more medals than the USSR in the 1980 and 1984 winter Olympics. The only interruption to communist victory was in 1968, when the USSR took second place to Norway in winter and to the USA in summer, and in the summer of 1984 when the major communist sporting nations did not compete.

One overriding problem facing the German Democratic Republic after the war was that of gaining international acceptance as an independent state. Its leaders further had to contend with attempts to impose Soviet institutions and values upon the country, on the one hand, and Western hostility, subversion and boycott on the other. The rivalry with the Federal Republic of Germany was evidently to become a testing ground for proving the viability of either capitalism or socialism in all spheres, including sport. After 1949, as a leading East German sports historian has written, the GDR was confronted with 'the challenge of the mass media and sports organisations of the Federal Republic which, exploiting the higher standards of sport in West Germany, were claiming superiority and defaming the GDR'.[25]

Success in sport was seen in the GDR as one means, perhaps the most accessible and 'popular', of gaining acceptance of the regime and enhancing its image at home and abroad while other channels were closed. It was not easy. In the winter Olympics of 1960, for example, the USA refused visas to GDR athletes to travel to Squaw Valley where the Games were being held. Such denial of visas was made 35 times by the USA and its NATO allies between 1957 and 1967. In other instances, when GDR athletes won competitions, the awards ceremony was cancelled; and often Western officials refused permission for the GDR to display its flag and emblem at victory ceremonies.

But the GDR persisted, continuing to win international titles and to host European and world championships. It is impossible to make any study of GDR sport without seeing it in the wider context of, first, striving to establish the nation as the equal of its fellow German state, the Federal Republic and, second, trying to achieve both political and sporting status in the world, above all within the Olympic movement and the United Nations. It is a measure of the success of these objectives that final acceptance by the IOC came in 1972, for the Games significantly held in the Federal Republic of Germany (Munich), to be followed the following year by membership of the United Nations. Both were the result of 25 years of intensive diplomatic activity, sporting and political.

Although the IOC had recognised the National Olympic Committee of the GDR in October 1965 and granted it the right to enter a team separately from West Germany in the Mexico Olympics of 1968, it was only in Munich in 1972 that the GDR for the first time possessed its own national team, flag and anthem. This sporting autonomy and success led to mounting diplomatic recognition of the GDR throughout the world. Table 5 shows the steady change-round in Olympic success between the two German states. While West Germany was overwhelmingly successful in the 1950s, the gap closed in the 1960s, then East Germany forged well ahead in the 1970s and 1980s.

Table 5 *Olympic results, GDR and FRG, 1952–88*

Games	GDR				FRG			
	Gold	Silver	Bronze	Total	Gold	Silver	Bronze	Total
1952 Summer	–	–	–	–	0	7	17	24
Winter	–	–	–	–	3	2	2	7
1956 Summer	1	4	2	7	5	9	6	20
Winter	0	0	1	1	1	0	0	1
1960 Summer	3	9	7	19	10	10	6	26
Winter	2	1	0	3	2	2	1	5
1964 Summer	3	7	6	16	7	15	12	34
Winter	2	2	0	4	1	0	3	4
1968 Summer	9	9	7	25	5	10	10	25
Winter	1	2	2	5	2	2	3	7
1972 Summer	20	23	23	66	13	11	16	40
Winter	4	3	7	14	3	1	1	5
1976 Summer	40	25	25	90	10	12	17	39
Winter	7	5	7	19	2	5	3	10
1980 Summer	47	37	42	126	–	–	–	–
Winter	9	7	7	23	0	2	3	5
1984 Summer	–	–	–	–	17	19	23	59
Winter	9	9	6	24	2	1	1	4
1988 Summer	37	35	30	103	11	14	15	40
Winter	9	10	6	25	2	4	2	8

It is not only in the Olympic Games that the GDR established itself as one of the top two nations; it also became the world's foremost nation in track and field and swimming. In the Second World Track and Field Championships, held in Rome in 1987, the GDR gained the highest medal tally with 31 (USSR 25, USA 19), including 10 gold medals (USSR 7, USA 9). Success in swimming is even more marked. In the 1986 World Championships, GDR men won 1 gold, 4 silver and 1 bronze medal, while GDR women took gold in all 14 disciplines, as well as 8 silver and 3 bronze! At European level, in 1983, the GDR women's performance was unprecedented: they took first and second place in *every* event, and won both relays. In Olympic and world championship terms, calculated in per capita medals, the GDR has in the past decade won 1 gold medal for every 425,000 citizens, by contrast with approximately 1 gold per 6,500,000 in the USA and USSR. In short this means that a GDR citizen with sports talent and ability has been 16 times more likely to reach the top and gain an Olympic or world gold medal than a person in either the USA or USSR.

For the German Democratic Republic, therefore, we have seen how, to quote a West German source,

> Sport has played a vital role in breaching the blockade which, at the time of the Cold War, kept the GDR out of virtually all international relations outside the communist states. Because GDR sport attained international standards and in many areas actually set those standards, world sports organisations were unable to ignore the country.[26]

This was an important step towards helping the GDR break out of its political isolation, gain credibility for the government with its own people, and be recognised as an independent German state. Hence the high priority that the GDR authorities accorded the development of sport and international sports performance.

Although not as spectacular, the evolution of Cuban and Chinese sport, since 1960 and 1984 respectively, has been dominated by similar considerations – of international recognition and prestige.

The communist countries therefore have been keenly aware of the advantages that are thought to accrue from sporting, and especially Olympic, success, and prepare their athletes accordingly. They believe that the Olympics bring more exposure and prestige, and are, in the view of some communist leaders, *the* measure of a national's viability.

Some conclusions

With its control of the sports system, the communist leadership has been able to mobilise resources to use sport to perform what it believes to be salient political functions in foreign policy. As we have seen, this includes promoting neighbourly relations with bordering and geo-politally strategic states; it also includes winning support for communist states, their policies and form of socialism (e.g. Soviet v Chinese) among developing states in Africa, Asia and Latin America. It is, of course, impossible to measure the impact of sport on the behaviour of states – to discover whether sport can, in fact, ever affect policies, let alone minds and hearts.

All that can be said is that sport would no longer seem to be (if it ever was) the neutral, apolitical medium that some people once considered it. Certainly, communist leaders have never had any illusion that sport is neutral:

> Neutrality of sport is a mystification. Sport and politics have always been interwined . . . The idea of peaceful coexistence between countries with different political systems is, in the nuclear age, the only alternative to world destruction. International sport and the Olympic movement have by their universal nature enormous potential for being an important vehicle in imple-menting that idea.[27]

The sporting gains of communist policy towards developing and neighbouring countries are evident and tangible. The political gains, however, are far from certain. There have been successes in the 'hearts and minds' campaign among such nations, but the staunchness of friendship and solidarity remains open to question: for example, very few developing states showed solidarity with the Soviet-led boycott of the Los Angeles Games in 1984 or, indeed, with the Soviet armed involvement in Afghanistan. Some might argue, further, that Western commercial sport seems to have had more of an impact on the popular imagination in Africa, Asia and Latin America than have communist- and Olympic-style sports. It may be that, as far as communist influence is concerned, communist policy is most effective where Marxist–Leninist assumptions are accepted, in a handful of communist countries themselves. Like the space programme, it seems more important in establishing national pride and ideological hegemony, though it appears to have markedly less impact outside of states that are already Marxist–Leninist and, in recent times, even that bastion has crumbled.

All the same, it is undeniable that the considerable and multifarious forms of sports aid to developing states by the economically advanced communist countries have won friends and allies. That communist relations with the Olympic movement are in general subordinate to the general lines of communist foreign policy is indisputable, and this has led on occasion to political opportunism. But it is equally true that sport and the Olympic movement have assumed, as a result, a pre-eminent role in moral leadership in the context of world politics.

Notes

1 Y. A. Talayev, 'Sport – oblast mirnovo sorevnovaniya', *Teoriya i praktika fizicheskoi kultury*, no. 1, 1973, p. 8.
2 Max Beloff, *The Foreign Policy of Soviet Russia, 1929–1941*, vol. 2 (Oxford University Press, Oxford, 1947), p. 5.
3 Leon Trotsky, in Jan Meijer (ed.), *The Trotsky Papers, 1917–1922*, vol. 1 (Paladine Press, New York, 1964), p. 623.
4 J. V. Stalin, *Voprosy Leninizma* (Politizdat, Moscow, 1947), p. 179.
5 V. Balashov, 'Sport i vneshnyaya politika', *Teoriya i praktika fizicheskoi kultury*, no. 3, 1971, p. 5.
6 See David Lane, *State and Politics in the USSR* (Basil Blackwell, Oxford, 1985), p. 90.
7 Editorial in *Sovetsky sport*, 1 December 1981, p. 1.
8 He Zhangleang, 'Soviet–Chinese ties', *Soviet Weekly*, 7 March 1987, p. 14.
9 V. Ivanov, 'Sportivnye otnosheniya', *Sport v SSSR*, no. 11, 1970, p. 14.
10 A. Prokhorov, 'Nam nuzhny vashi spetsialisty', *Sport v SSSR*, no. 6, 1972, p. 24.
11 Editorial in *Sport v SSSR*, no. 6, 1981, p. 39.
12 Konstantin Andrianov, 'Sovetskie respubliki i mezhdunarodnoye razvitie sportivnykh otnosheniy', *Fizkultura i sport*, no. 3, 1971, p. 1.
13 F. Iordanskaya, 'Novye sportivnye soglasheniya', *Sovetsky sport*, 22 October 1979, p. 3.
14 S. Orlova, 'Sovetsky mnogonatsionalny sport', *Sportivnaya zhizn Rossii*, no. 11, 1972, p. 7.
15 A. O. Romanov, *Mezhdunarodnoye sportivnoye dvizhenie* (Fizkultura i sport, Moscow, 1973), p. 177.
16 *Ibid.*, p. 90.
17 Fidel Castro, *El Deporte*, no. 3, 1976, p. 9.
18 Editorial in *Pravda*, 17 September 1972, p. 1.
19 Erich Honecker, *Report of the Central Committee to the Ninth Congress of the Socialist Unity Party of Germany* (Berlin, 1976), p. 133.
20 Y. A. Talayev, 'Sport – oblast mirnovo sorevnovaniya', *Teoriya i praktika fizicheskoi kultury*, no. 1, 1973, p. 8.
21 Fidel Castro, in S. Castanes (ed.), *Fidel. Sobre el deporte* (El Deporte, Havana, 1974), p. 91.
22 See *Kultura i zhizn*, 1 November 1949, p. 5.
23 *Ibid.*
24 See the *Avery Brundage Collection*, Letter No. 149: 'Private and Confidential,' p. 2.
25 Günther Wonneberger, 'Arbeitersport in der DDR', in A. Krüger and J. Riordan (eds), *Der internationale Arbeitersport* (Pahl-Rugenstein, Cologne, 1985), p. 17.

26 See *Sport in der Deutschen Demokratischen Republik* (Friedrich-Ebert-Stiftung, Bonn, 1975), pp. 12–13.
27 P. Kats, 'Sport i "neitralitet" ', *Teoriya i praktika fizicheskoi kultury*, no. 3, 1979, pp. 54–55.

Chapter Nine
Trends and transformations

During the latter part of the 1980s glasnost-inspired liberalisation in most of Eastern Europe – though not in many communist states beyond the European continent – brought radical changes to communist sport. These changes are breaking the mould of its state-controlled utilitarian (plan-fulfilment) structure. In a way the changes illustrate the diminishing ability of sport bureaucrats to enforce Stalinist norms established during the late 1920s in the USSR and after the Second World War elsewhere. They are also a response to the limitations inflicted on athletes and society by the requirements of high-performance sport.

The Soviet sports minister (or, to give him his proper title, Chairman of the USSR State Sports Committee) has admitted that 'Our sports ministry has indeed been oriented primarily on attaining prestigious victories in international tournaments'. In response to changes elsewhere in Eastern Europe and to pressure from below, he promised that 'Gradually concern for promoting both sport for all and high-performance sport will shift to independent federations. With time the Sports Committee will concentrate its efforts on training and retraining personnel, on the social protection of athletes and the provision of sports facilities.'[1]

A picture of communist sport would therefore be incomplete without mention of recent trends and likely transformations.

In the early 1980s it was China that began the process of transformation in sport. It increasingly oriented its sports policy on the West, chiefly the USA, opening up the country to commercial sport for leisure and recreation – from golf and baseball to women's body-building, boxing and weight-lifting.[2] At the same time, it started to pay more attention to hitherto neglected groups and sports, such as the disabled and the folk-games of national minorities.[3] such processes in China prompted, after March 1985, a reappraisal of sport in the Soviet Union and this, in turn, inspired similar reappraisals throughout Eastern Europe.

In so far as it is the Soviet policies of perestroika, glasnost and democratisation – including those in sport – that have had considerable reverberations within the communist world, this final chapter is largely concerned with them and their implications for communist and world sport generally.

Since Mikhail Gorbachev took charge of Soviet politics in March 1985, no area of society, sport included, has been immune to what he himself calls a new revolution. However, it has to be understood that while the coming of a new man has accelerated the process of change, it was opposition from below to the old regime and mounting disaffection from official values and institutions that initiated it and carried it forward. The following would seem to be the major trends in Soviet sport in the late 1980s and early 1990s.

Sport for all

The Soviet leadership has always maintained in public that *massovost* (mass participation) takes precedence over *masterstvo* (proficiency or elite sport), and down the years it has produced regiments of statistics to prove the case: that millions are regular, active participants in sport, that the vast majority of school and college students gain a GTO badge, that rising millions (a third of the population) take part in the spartakiads, that the bulk of workers do their daily dozen – the 'production gymnastics' – at the workplace.

We now learn in this 'honesty's the best policy' era that these figures were fraudulent and a show to impress people above and below and to meet preset targets (each school, region, factory and farm received a sports quota and incurred penalties and criticism if they fell short). It is now admitted that only 8% of men and 2% of women engage in sport regularly.[4]

It is further revealed that when put to the test only 41 out of 700 Moscow schoolchildren taking part in a city sports tournament could meet the GTO requirements, and only 0.5% of the capital's 11-year-olds met GTO standards.[5] Even among men doing their national service, as many as a third could not meet the norms.[6]

Although swimming is an obligatory element in the GTO programme, it appears that only 11% of schoolchildren can swim and fewer than 5% pass the GTO swimming norm.[7] Even in a Republic with a Californian climate, Armenia, most youngsters cannot swim.[8]

All college and university students must attend two weekly sessions of physical exercise and sport during their first academic year; yet a survey at Moscow State University discovered that only some 17% were physically fit. The conclusion drawn was that compulsion results in resistance and anti-sport sentiments.[9]

For most people sport remains out of reach: some two-thirds of workers are not members of any sports organisation and 'their physical fitness makes only a tiny contribution to raising productivity, reducing the sickness rate and resolving social and economic problems'.[10]

Significantly, the 1986 Spartakiad passed off in a low-key manner with no participation figures released for the first time since the Games were held. There are even signs that the GTO programme, for long the bedrock of the sports and fitness system, is being abandoned, partly out of a desire to break with the past 'fiddling of the books' and partly from its increasing unpopularity with teachers parents and pupils. A serious start to involve more young people in casual sport was made back in 1981 when the government decreed that sports schools (clubs) should not be confined to gifted athletes.[11] Yet subsequent reports frequently complained of coaches and sports centre managers trying to keep ordinary youngsters out.

The next step therefore was to depart from the hallowed principle of completely free sport by introducing charges for the use of pool, gym, court and stadium; that, at least, it was thought, might induce amenity owners to open their doors. Further, with official permission in 1987 for co-operative ventures to start up, a number of co-operative health, fitness and sports clubs began to appear. A health club opened in Moscow in mid-1988, charging three roubles as entrance fee and a scale of charges for various treatments and activities.[12] In Leningrad the Juventus Health and Sports Club had come into existence a few months earlier with activities ranging from aikido wrestling, skate-boarding and break-dancing to tennis, swimming and even weight-watching exercises. A month's membership costs ten roubles; the club had a regular membership of 600 within months of opening, and had another 800 on its waiting list.[13] A co-operative group in the town of Podolsk, some 50 km south of Moscow, had the bright idea of hiring out municipal sports facilities during 'fallow' time – evenings and week-ends; in 1988 it charged 1.30 roubles an hour for swimming, just under a rouble for an hour's use of sports grounds and 2.20 roubles for a two-hour sauna session.[14] At the same time in the southern Republic of

Georgia, the one-time tennis star Alex Metreveli opened a string of tennis clubs along the Black Sea coast and in the Georgian capital of Tbilisi.[15]

A major change has also come over the trade union sports societies: in mid-1987 the eight leading societies (including Spartak, Lokomotiv and Vodnik) amalgamated to form a single sports organisation in an attempt to improve facilities and service to the public as well as to 'democratise the work of sports clubs'. They also declared their intention of reducing top-level leagues and competitions so as to divert more funds to sport for all and to cater for a diversity of interest groups and health clubs.[16]

At school the physical education programme has been adjusted to make some form of recreation a daily feature for all children and to provide a choice of activity.[17] And in higher education, students can now choose the times at which they engage in their compulsory sports activity, and they have a wider range of options.

Much remains to be done, as Soviet periodicals readily attest. But even if the sports establishment is fighting a rearguard battle, at least many problems have been identified and something is being done to tackle them.

Independent clubs

Young people have not sat around in the last decade awaiting Party or government resolutions. In fact, a major impulse for official action has come from young people turning their backs on officially recommended activities and on official organisations, like the Young Pioneers and the Young Communist League (which lost 10 million of its 40 million members in just five years from 1985 to 1990)[18], and they have been forming their own groups and clubs. Although initially illegal, since only officially sanctioned groups have been permitted in the USSR, the authorities seemed unable or unwilling to suppress them. Finally, in May 1986, the government set the official seal on their existence by changing the law.[19]

In the field of sport, the clubs range from soccer fan clubs to groups for sports for which the government has been slow to provide facilities: aerobics, yoga, body-building, jogging, and karate and other combat sports. One of the first independent groups were soccer fans in the late 1970s and early 1980s, especially of Moscow Spartak, with their own distinctive red-and-white home-knitted scarves and hats. They were followed by combat sports clubs for both defence and offence in the spreading street and soccer gang clashes. One of the more sinister groups is that known as the Lyubery, a Rambo-style youth gang that started several years ago in the Moscow 'smoke-stack' suburb of Lyubertsy and then spread to other urban, and especially suburban, centres. These male teenage toughs tend to be obsessed with martial arts and body-building, constructing their own gyms in the basements of blocks of flats.[20]

The forced acceptance of such independent clubs is a radical departure for the Soviet authorities; after all, no groups free of Party or Party agency tutelage have been tolerated since the 1920s. Perhaps the current leadership is responding to Trotsky's warning after the 1917 Revolution that:

> The longing for amusement, distraction, recreation and fun is the most legitimate desire of human nature . . . We must make sure this longing is given full rein and freed from the guardianship of the pedagogue and the tiresome habit of moralising.[21]

Women and sport

Up and down the USSR women have long ignored the pontification of male leaders about their participation in 'harmful' sports – soccer, body-building, ice hockey, judo, weight-lifting, water polo and long-distance running. As recently as 1973 the USSR Sports Committee issued a resolution discouraging women from taking part in sports that were allegedly harmful to the female organism and encouraged male voyeurism. Women's soccer, for example, was said to be 'injurious to a woman's organism . . . Physical stress typical of playing soccer can cause harm to sexual functions, varicose veins, thrombo-phlebitis and so on.'[22] What the resolution did not explain was why playing soccer was harmless for men, or why those ailments did not result from approved (Olympic) sports like field hockey and basketball.

Within the space of a few years, however, Soviet women have held four national judo competitions and a world judo championship, and as many as 15,000 women are registered in judo clubs.[23] The first women's national soccer championships were held in August 1987, sponsored by the campaigning youth weekly *Sobesednik*. Moscow University formed its first women's water-polo team back in 1982; the women's sport has now spread to several other cities and the Soviet women's team played its first international fixture (against Hungary) in 1987. Weight-lifting and body-building are developing apace: the first women's body-building championship was held in Tyumen in 1988, and women have been members of body-building clubs in the Baltic Republics at least since 1986. Women's ice hockey has reappeared for the first time since the 1920s, and women are doing the marathon, pole-vault, triple-jump and hammer.

These changes have all come about by a few women defying official sanction, ridicule and even persecution to establish their right to pursue the sport of their choice.

Sport and the disabled

Another disadvantaged group to benefit from the wind of change is the handicapped, long neglected by the Soviet sport establishment. It is now admitted that, 'For a long time we pretended the problem did not exist. We thought: the state looks after the handicapped, social security provides living and working conditions for them. What else do they want?'[24]

Before 1988 the USSR had never held domestic championships at any level for any category of handicapped person. Two years after China had staged its first nation-wide games for the handicapped and in the year of the Seoul Paralympics, the newly formed Invalid Sports Federation held its inaugural championships in the Estonian capital of Tallinn. This was the culmination of long years of campaigning by pressure groups, recently joined by thousands of maimed ex-Afghanistan veterans. While, again, it is the Baltic Republics (Estonia, Latvia and Lithuania) that are clearly in the forefront of providing facilities for the physically and mentally handicapped, elsewhere conditions are plainly woeful. Even 'Moscow has no equipment, coach, doctor, or sports facilities for the disabled'.[25]

After a number of well-publicised complaints that 'sport for the disabled has been developing around the world with virtually no participation from the Soviet Union',[26] a team of invalid athletes was sent to the Olympics for the very first time, to Seoul in October 1988. Unlike their able-bodied compatriots in the Olympic Games, who won 55 golds and 132 medals overall – a quarter of all Olympic medals – the 13 blind athletes making up the Soviet disabled team won no medals at all. But at least a start has been made.

As well as movement towards caring more for minorities, the Soviet government is also showing signs of encouraging folk-game festivals, especially among the non-Russian nationalities (which now together outnumber Russians in the population of the USSR).[27]

Changing the image of Soviet sport

The sudden spate of honesty and the broaching of previously unmentionable (censored) subjects have revealed the dark side of the Soviet sport and stirred up considerable debate. Journalists now talk frankly about occasional match-fixing in the major spectator sports, bribery of referees, drug-taking and other nefarious activities hitherto only mentioned in the context of capitalist sport. They have also raised questions about the very fundamentals of communist sport: its ethos and ethics.

In an article entitled 'It is people who lose' and backed by a full-page caricature of two muscle-bound colossuses carrying a winner's podium over the heads of a host of casual athletes, a journalist derided the 'win at all costs' mentality and privileges for the elite. He recalled the pentathlete Boris Onishchenko caught cheating in the Montreal Olympics: 'Did his coach really know nothing? Did the sports leadership subject him to public ostracism?'[28]

He went on to mention two Soviet weight-lifters caught selling anabolic steroids in Canada (taken *out of* the USSR). The problem of drugs has also been raised in the press and on TV by two respected ex-athletes and prominent sports officials: the weight-lifter Yuri Vlasov and the long-jumper Igor Ter-Ovanesyan (see Chapter 7).

A year after Vlasov's live TV accusations the daily sports paper *Sovetsky sport* claimed that Oleg Solovyov, coach to Novosibirsk's top swimmers, had encouraged the use of anabolic steroids in training sessions.[29] Subsequently, following the Seoul Olympics and the Ben Johnson drug scandal, Soviet senior track-and-field coach Igor Ter-Ovanesyan launched a well-publicised campaign against drug-taking in Soviet sport. Admitting that 'many of our athletes' take drugs, he conceded that even several school athletes had been caught taking steroids; and he advised, 'that society needs proper legislation to combat this evil, seriously punishing both athletes and doctors, coaches and the drug suppliers'.[30] Other sources have uncovered drug-taking in Soviet cycling, rowing, weight-lifting and body-building.

Another stone overturned by investigative journalists is that of 'amateur' status. It has to be said in parenthesis that the Soviet leadership only introduced 'state amateur status' into Soviet sport in the early 1950s, under IOC pressure, as a ploy to join the Olympic movement (the USSR was accepted in May 1951). From then on the appearance had to be given that performers received no remuneration from their sports performance, nor did they devote themselves full-time to sport. The public, of course, knew differently, but it was part of the double-think of the 1950–85 period never to mention it in public. Glasnost is drawing aside the veil. As the youth monthly *Yunost* has put it,

> We got used to living a double life because many of our idols did the same. We condemned professional sport in the West and were proud that our champions were amateurs. We were expected to assume that our athletes trained for six or seven hours each day after work or study. But everyone knew that most athletes never went to work or college classes, and that they met their workmates or fellow students only on pay day.[31]

It is now officially revealed that top soccer players receive a basic salary of 200–300 roubles a month for playing soccer (average industrial earnings being some 200 roubles), and spend as many as 250 days annually in training.[32]

Journalists have also broached other once-censored topics, like the security service sponsorship of Dinamo and the army officer sinecures for athletes sponsored by the armed forces.[33]

Under pressure, the sports establishment has talked of steps to make sports, especially soccer, clubs self-financing and officially to give all players of Master of Sport ranking and over what they have always had unofficially: professional status. This naturally follows the amendment to Olympic regulations that permits professional performers in the Games. By 1990, however, no firm decision on the latter issue had been taken, although a few soccer clubs have become self-financing and openly professional. The first, the hitherto undistinguished provincial club Dnepr, not only became Soviet league champions in 1988 but made a handsome profit into the bargain. In the 1989 soccer season, the second division club Metallurg of Zaporozhe followed suit, introducing individual and collective membership (8 and 5000 roubles annually respectively), which, it hopes, will generate over a million roubles.[34] Similarly, a 14-strong team of Soviet cyclists signed a contract in late 1988 with the San Marino aluminium firm Alfa Lum to form the first-ever professional Soviet cycling team under contract to a foreign company (with the USSR Sports Committee taking a third of their earnings).[35] Perhaps the greatest volte-face in sporting principles is the entry of Soviet boxers and wrestlers into the professional ranks.[36]

Fears are being voiced, none the less, that the encouragement of open professionalism might spoil the 'stars' even more than at present. It is nostalgically recalled that once upon a time Soviet athletes would go through hell to gain medals. 'That was before the good mother Adidas fed them from her bountiful bosom, spoiled them with life on the foreign circuit or even overseas training.' Today's athletes, however, are 'scientifically programmed, rigged out in the latest fashions and packed full of home-produced "vitamins"; as a result, we have produced capricious idols and we know not what to do with them.'[37] The dilemma is not Soviet alone.

The morality of professional sport

A logical extension of the debate on the future of Soviet sport is seriously to question the morality of top-class sport today. A number of articles in the press have 'only recently started to mention out loud the major problem [in sport] – deception, the rust that begins to corrode a child's innocent mind from that sacred moment when the first mischievous thought clouds the pure joy of playing – that besides enjoying himself, he can make something out of it'.[38]

This brings us to a basic question that was raised frequently in the 1920s, yet has rarely been aired since: what price is society prepared to pay for talent? How wide should the gap in privileges be between the stars and the masses? Should a communist society encourage the formation of an elite based on the luck of nature's draw and thereby perpetuate original inequalities rather than properly compensating for the lottery of birth?

Such fundamental questions (to a socialist society) are certainly being asked now. The following extract faces squarely up to the problem:

> From a youngster's first steps in sport he is accustomed to being a parasite, clandestinely assigned to miners, oilers or builders who generously repay his artless 'feints' with worldly goods of which the miner, oiler or builder can only dream. City apartments, cars, overseas trips, a free and easy life by the seaside – how that all caresses youthful vanity, lifts him above the grey mass of those who have been waiting years for housing, phones and cars, and who have to pay for the seaside and foreign trips out of their own pocket.[39]

Besides criticising the perverted morality that permits such privilege, a number of Soviet writers have also called into question the exploitation of children for the sake of irrational glory. A sports monthly has written of the 'strict regimentation and deprivation of many of childhood's joys, the numerous trips, lengthy training camps, hotel stays, separations from family and school . . . all this leads to moral impairment'.[40]

Yet when Yuri Vlasov complained of the 'inhuman forms of profes-sionalism' involving 12- and 13-year-old youngsters, especially in gym-nastics and swimming, he was accused by Soviet coaches of 'under-mining Soviet sport'. Disillusioned, he quit his post as Chairman of the Weight-lifting Federation and returned to writing fiction.[41]

All the same, more and more critics are taking up the cudgels against intensive training of children at the age of 5, 6 or 7, especially after the publication of a study of children's sports schools in Kazan, showing that 'there was practically no difference between beginners and top athletes when it came to the number of intensive training sessions'.[42]

The mood of glasnost appears more to favour sport for all than special privileges for the gifted.

Convergence in sport

Yet another consequence of Gorbachev's new policies seems to be the bringing closer of some facets of Soviet sport to those in the West; it is none the less a contradictory process that may have popular acclaim, yet at the same time lead Soviet sport further away from the new morality it seeks.

For a start, commercial sports (in a professional, commodity sense) like golf, baseball, Grand Prix motor-racing, even dog-racing, have arrived in the USSR. Moscow had its first (nine-hole) golf course in 1988, partly designed for the foreign diplomatic corps and partly intended to prepare Soviet challengers for international golf tournaments (60 teenagers were registered at the club's golf school). The American billionaire Armand Hammer was planning a second golf course at Nakhabino, some 30 km from the centre of Moscow.[43] With an eye to the inclusion of baseball in the Olympic Games, the sports establishment has 'created' Soviet baseball clubs (just as it 'created' field hockey teams by fiat in the early 1970s expressly for Olympic participation – again without any grass-roots tradition); the first baseball league came into being in 1988, a year after the first national championships. By late 1988 there were 30 baseball clubs in the country and a special children's baseball school in Tashkent in Soviet Central Asia.[44]

Following the holding of the first Grand Prix Formula 1 race in a communist country, Hungary, in 1988, the Soviet Union is now designing a world-class track in the Moscow Region with a view to hosting Formula 1 racing; and *Pravda* has called for the promotion of Soviet motor-racing up to world standards.[45] Further, the USSR Sports

Committee has expressed an interest in staging a Dallas Cowboys v. Washington Redskins football game in Moscow's Lenin Stadium; the first Soviet American football team, the Moscow Bears, came into existence in late 1989, backed by the Moscow Young Communist League.[46]

To cap it all, the first dog races (for borzois) were held at the Moscow Hippodrome (normally used for horse-racing) in the autumn of 1987. Borzoi-racing had been a popular pastime of the Russian gentry prior to 1917. As a concession to the public, horse-racing in all forms (trotting, hurdling, steeplechase and racing on the flat – with gambling on the state totalisator) has existed for most of the Soviet period, even though 'no mention of it had been made in the press, simply because it was not accepted practice'. Nor had it ever featured on TV, despite the country's 3000 racehorses and 17 annual race meetings.[47]

Other recent 'imports' include snooker, wushu or Chinese 'shadow-boxing' (as many as 52 cities are said to have wushu clubs with over 30,000 members[48]), and Western-style body-building – the first international body-building contest, watched by 16,000 spectators, was held in Moscow in late 1988, jointly sponsored by the German Armstrong Company and the USSR Sports Committee.[49] It was even planned to stage bullfighting in Moscow in the Lenin Stadium, with over 30 pedigree bulls being brought from Madrid for the spectacle during 1990. However, public outrage successfully averted the blood-letting and forced the organisers (including, once again, the Young Communist League, eager to boost profits for its functionaries) to cancel the show.[50]

If all that were not enough to turn past policies on their heads, the USSR Sports Committee signed a contract with the Italian firm Ocrim Spa to sponsor all six Soviet soccer teams in European competitions in the 1987–88 season; the teams wore the Ocrim logo in all matches during the season. This prompted other sports teams and federations to seek sponsorship from both foreign and Soviet firms. As a result, 'the National Olympic Committee has set up a federation of sponsors to coordinate commercial activity in the interests of Soviet sport and of strengthening ties abroad'.[51]

Another innovation in Soviet sport, bringing it in line with Western practices, is to sell leading Soviet players to Western teams. Initially, in 1987, these were players of 30 and over; subsequently, younger men were sold when the price was right. Players included Lavrentiev, Ladygin, Kapustin and Shalimov in ice hockey, Blokhin, Zavarov, Dasayev, Baltacha and Shalva in soccer, and Ended, Sabonis, Volkov and Kurtinaitis in basketball. By 1990 as many as 30 ice-hockey players had signed for the North American National Hockey League.[52] As an example of such an arrangement, the Soviet national team goalkeeper Rinat Dasayev signed a $2 million contract for two years with the Spanish club Sevilla; the USSR Sports Committee took 55% of the proceeds, Dasayev's club Spartak received 40%, and the Italian agents Dorna, who set up the deal, took 5%.[53] The striker Zavarov, however, was sold to Juventus in Italy for $5 million, with his former club Dinamo Kiev gaining $2 million from the transfer.[54]

In view of the admittance of some of the top professional basketball players to the Olympics, Soviet basketball teams have begun to play against top US professionals, and Soviet players have been sold to US teams. Furthermore, discussions were underway in early 1989 for a Soviet ice-hockey team to compete in the North American Ice Hockey League (for the Stanley Cup). Negotiations were also being held with a Canadian sponsor for Soviet boxers (24 were candidates) to box professionally in Western rings.

It may well be that the spirit of openness will soon persuade the sports leadership to accept open competition in all sporting contests, including the Olympics, and to declare all Soviet top-level athletes as practising professionals. It is now admitted that today some 90,000 Soviet athletes are full-time professionals.[55] Professionalisation may signify an end to bureaucratic interference in sport; it may also contribute to the independence and dignity of athletes, coaches, sports organisers and journalists (who no longer have to pretend professionals are amateurs). However, as the history of Western sport has shown, professionalism in sport represents a set of practices that can be every bit as pernicious and unhealthy as they may be liberating and healthy. In the Soviet Union today, no one – fans, officials, players, or journalists – wishes to see the Soviet domestic leagues become merely a farm system for the wealthiest clubs in Western Europe and North America.

The thorny issue of remuneration, especially when it concerns foreign currency, has excited acrimonious debate in the Soviet media – also for the first time, since this had previously been one of the many censored topics. On the one hand, state officials claimed that Soviet-trained stars had a civic and patriotic duty to devote the bulk of their foreign earnings to the benefit of Soviet sport generally. On the other hand, as the top male tennis player, Andrei Chesnokov, has put it, he earns lucrative foreign currency on the world tennis circuit, yet is permitted only $25 a day by the USSR Sports Committee – 'not enough even to feed myself'.[56] Some critics acuse officals of wasting huge sums of money 'on trips abroad for Sports Committee bosses and their retinue, on officials who needlessly accompany teams and on translators who in most cases are not needed'[57] (but who in the past were often employed to 'keep an eye' on athletes abroad and to report back to the KGB on returning home).

The Sports Committee is also accused of going 'on a hard currency spending spree when it badly wants athletes to win'. At the Calgary Winter Olympics in 1988, for example, each Soviet gold medal winner 'received $5000 no matter how strong their rivals were'.[58] For a gold medal at the Seoul Olympics in the same year, the Soviet Sports Minister admitted that Soviet recipients would gain 12,000 roubles (Rb 6000 for silver and Rb 4000 for bronze). Since the Soviet squad won 55 gold medals and 132 medals overall, the Sports Committee spent about a million roubles, much of it in foreign currency, in bonuses alone.[59]

Under pressure, sports officials have also revealed that it cost a minimum of $180,000 to guarantee participation of Soviet players and coaches in the 1990 world ice-hockey championships. The players and coaches who gained second place in Europe and first place in the world received an average of $6000 each. For the World Cup in Italy in July 1990, a sum of $1.5 million was set aside; if Soviet soccer players had won the Cup they would each have received $30,000.

Not everyone in the USSR is happy at what is seen as a race for false glory, as the cultivation of irrational loyalties, as unreasonable prominence given to the winning of victories, the setting of records and the collection of trophies – the obsessive fetishism of present-day sport. In fact, one of the features of popular antipathy to the pre-Gorbachev 'stagnation' period was precisely a reaction against the tub-thumping, flag-waving concern with international sports success. As a writer in *Sobesednik* wrote before the Seoul Olympics,

> International prestige is important, but what is more so is to involve ordinary people in sport, to use Olympic success to attract the public into regular sporting activity and to ensure we have facilities for them. So don't let us spend too much time on celebrations, we must look down from the Olympic heights upon the realities of the world about us.[61]

Immediately following the 1988 Summer Olympics, a political commentator suggested that the Soviet media publish two sets of tables: one for Olympic medals and one for per capita provision of sports amenities by each nation. If that were done, the USSR 'would be in a very different position in the [second] table'. The writer cited the example of indoor skating rinks: Canada had 10,000, the USA 1500, Sweden 343 and the USSR just 102. Calling for 'new thinking' in sport, he went on,

> Not so long ago statistics were so 'cleverly' compiled that it seemed the entire population went in for sport . . . Can't we see for ourselves that much more emphasis is being put on professional sport, on training record breakers, champions, medal winners than on sport for all?[62]

The issue is complex, and by no means unfamiliar to other states. But the implications of popular pressure reacting against the 'excesses' and plain deception of the past may well force the Soviet sports and political leadership to put less emphasis in future on striving for international success and more on satisfying popular desire for a wide range of fun and games.

If popular pressure and changing official priorities have combined to reduce the Soviet commitment to international success through sport (already visible in the relative poor showing of Soviet athletes at the 1990 European Track and Field Championships in Split, where the USSR trailed behind East Germany and Great Britain), they have made a dramatic impact on the sports systems in the six countries of Eastern Europe that cast aside their communist regimes in 1989 – Bulgaria, Czechoslovakia, East Germany, Hungary, Poland and Romania). In the case of the German Democratic Republic, the unification with West Germany in October 1990 meant the disappearance of East Germany as a separate team from the world's arenas. Yet even before the demise of a separate East German sport, the new regime had disbanded the former sports administration and cut off virtually all funding to elite sports establishments. So parlous was the financial plight of East German athletes and teams in 1990 that they had to seek Western sponsorship in order to fulfil their commitments abroad. None the less, it is an indication of the eagerness with which West German political and sports leaders view the future united German sports challenge that East Germany was enabled to send a full team to the European Track and Field Championships and defeat the rest of Europe with ease. But the individual sports sponsorship of top stars has been growing in recent years and expresses the irrepressible rise of Western-style individualism in sport and the independence that financial security has given top Eastern European athletes – money certainly talks. It is likely that much of the infrastructure of the old East German sports system – the elite research and training programmes at the Leipzig German High School for Physical Culture, the sports medical rehabilitation centre at Kreischa, the sports boarding schools, and the coach training – will not only remain, but will be invigorated by West German funding.

In countries where, for the time being, a quasi-communist (socialist/ social-democratic) regime persists (Bulgaria and Romania), change is slower, as the old guard maintains its position in the sporting hierarchy, playing on the prestige and patriotism of international success through sport. This is in stark contrast with Czechoslovakia, Hungary and Poland where the new broom has swept away almost all the vestiges of the old Soviet-style sports system, decentralised sport, vastly reduced sports budgets and concentrated resources on recreation for the ordinary people, relying on local communities, voluntary assistance and self-financing clubs. All three countries have also tried to resurrect pre-communist national traditions and institutions: the pan-Slavist Sokol sport and gymnastics movement in Czechoslovakia and Poland; the Scouts, Ramblers and Roman Catholic sports clubs in Poland and Hungary; and separate Czech and Slovak clubs and folk-games. In elite sport they have attempted to gain Western sponsorship for staging prestigious events, like Formula 1 motor-racing in Hungary and tennis championships in Czechoslovakia; and the regimes have allowed top athletes to sell themselves to the highest foreign bidders without any age restriction.

Concluding words

Today, the inheritors of the sports system evolved during the Stalin, Khrushchev and Brezhnev years find themselves in a quandary: to what extent should they break with the past? How sharply and through what new forms should change be brought about? In the field of culture, and specifically of physical culture, how ought they dismantle the various by-now well-entrenched fetishised institutions and values?

The problem is circumscribed partly by the fact that Soviet and other communist leaders still evidently regard sport as an important weapon in the rivalry between East and West. The international situation is just one of a number of objective impediments (also including domestic economic, cultural and political factors, not to mention relations *within* the communist community) on leaders attempting to realise their desires – which in any case are likely to be by no means uniform or clearly perceived. Whatever course of action is pursued, the subjective will of leaders is bound to be constrained by the objective possibilities of the situation.

It could be argued that sport might continue to play what could be termed a Stalinist role well after the rest of society had ceased to resemble totalitarian structures. The administration of sport could remain a haven for those more comfortable with traditional values of control, order and discipline. As the Western experience has demonstrated, cultural hegemony can be an effective tool of social and political domination. Coercion may not be necessary if the forces of order can gain the consent of the subordinate classes.

It is possible that Soviet and communist sport generally will become a hybrid of the worst of both worlds, retaining the bureaucracy, instrumentalism and authoritarianism of the old ways and adding only the exploitation and corruption of some forms of Western sport. The final result will not inspire admiration. Much the same could be said of the larger reform processes now under way in the Soviet Union and elsewhere in Eastern Europe. Sport may not play a key role in determining the fate of the reforms, but its ultimate shape should tell us much about the success and failure of the socialist experiment.

Notes

1 Nikolai Rusak, 'Medali ili zdorovye?', *Argumenty i fakty*, 28 April–4 May 1990, p. 7.

2 See Ma Yihua, 'Friendship through golf', *China Sports*, 1988, no. 10, pp. 17–21; Z. Wubin, 'A rising sport in China', *China Sports*, 1985, no. 9, pp. 5–7; Xu Qi, 'Women's sports in China', *China Sports*, 1989, no. 3, pp. 2–15.

3 Zhao Chongqi, 'Minority people's sports meet', *China Sports*, 1986, no. 3, pp. 33–5: China staged its first Minority People's Folk Games in Beijing from 8 September to 20 October 1985; it attracted some 3000 participants from 30 ethnic groups.

4 Olga Dmitrieva, 'Bokal protiv detstvu', *Komsomolskaya pravda*, 8 June 1985, p. 2.

5 M. Kondratieva, 'Na uroke i v zhizni', *Molodoi kommunist*, 1986, no. 12, p. 74.

6 K. S. Demirchyan, 'O zadachakh respublikanskoi partiynoi organizatsii', *Kommunist*, 25 September 1984, p. 2.

7 S. Belits-Gelman, 'Lipa ne tonet', *Ogonyok*, 1987, no. 4, p. 27.

8 Demirchyan, p. 2.

9 B. Novikov, 'Ne zabudut li oni kak khodit?', *Sport v SSSR*, 1988, no. 3, p. 39.

10 V. Balashov, 'Proizvodstvennaya gimnastika i proizvoditelnost', *Sport v SSSR*, 1988, no. 7, p. 15.

11 Henceforth roughly half the 7,500 sports schools would be run by local councils and education authorities and open to all; the rest would be for gifted young athletes and controlled by Dinamo and the army clubs.

12 'Novy kooperativny klub zdorovya', *Moskovskie novosti*, 1988, no. 7, p. 14.

13 'New sports coop for Leningrad', *Soviet Weekly*, 7 May 1988, p. 14.

14 'Public gets coop sport dividend', *Soviet Weekly*, 18 June 1988, p. 18.

15 'Metreveli and co. open new tennis centres', *Soviet Weekly*, 22 October 1988, p. 16.

16 Balashov, p. 14.
17 See J. Riordan, 'School physical education in the Soviet Union', *Physical Education Review*, 1986, vol. 9, no. 2, p. 115.
18 See J. Riordan, 'The Komsomol in crisis', *Coexistence*, 1989, vol. 26, no. 3, p. 7.
19 For more details, see J. Riordan, 'Soviet youth: pioneers of change', *Soviet Studies*, 1988, vol. 15, no. 4, p. 560.
20 *Ibid.*, pp. 564–6.
21 Leon Trot.'ky, *Problems of Everyday Life* (Monad Press, New York, 1973), p. 32.
22 R. Davletshina, 'Futbol i zhenshchiny', *Teoriya i praktika fizicheskoi kultury*, 1973, no. 10, p. 62.
23 V. Merkulov, 'Pressing on regardless', *Soviet Weekly*, 17 October 1987, p. 16. Women were admitted to Soviet SAMBO (a form of judo) contests only in 1988, yet took 7 of the 10 gold medals in the 13th World Championships on their debut in 1990 (see *Soviet Weekly*, 31 May 1990, p. 16).
24 V. Ponomaryova, 'Yeshcho odna pobeda', *Sobesednik*, 1987, no. 37, p. 12.
25 *Ibid.*
26 S. Shenkman, 'Disabled sport: an end to bleeding hearts', *Soviet Weekly*, 11 June 1988, p. 16; see also *Sport v SSSR*, 1988, no. 5, pp. 50–2.
27 For example, a Russian troika championship was held in Krasnodar in 1986, and new emphasis has been given to the folk-games of Siberian peoples in the annual Sports Festival of the Peoples of the Far North (see *Soviet Weekly*, 6 September 1986, p. 11 and 1 November 1986, p. 14).
28 S. Tokarev, 'Ne proigral by chelovek', *Ogonyok*, 1987, no. 9, p. 20.
29 A. Klaz, 'Rekordy po retseptu', *Smena*, 4 May 1988, p. 3. See also Yuri Vlasov, 'Drugs and cruelty', *Moscow News*, 1988, no. 37, p. 15.
30 Igor Ter-Ovanesyan, 'I declare war on anabolics', *Moscow News*, 1988, no. 50, p. 15.
31 A. Novikov, 'Pismo redaktsii', *Yunost*, 1988, no. 10, p. 9.
32 Igor Oransky, 'Ne bogi gorshki obzhigayut . . .', *Moskovsky komsomolets*, 28 February 1989, p. 3.
33 O. Petrichenko, 'Ne sotvori sebe kumira', *Ogonyok*, 1987, no. 12, p. 15.
34 Oransky, p. 3.
35 M. Shlayev, 'Pervaya sovetskaya professionalnaya komanda', *Moskovskie novosti*, 1988, no. 50, p. 15; W. Fotheringham, 'Russian pros ready for taste of the Big Time', *Cycling Weekly*, 2 February 1989, pp. 8–9.
36 Mark Vodovozov, 'Borba na ringe', *Moskovskie novosti*, 15 January 1989, no. 3, p. 15; Oransky, p. 3.
37 Petrichenko, p. 15.
38 *Ibid.*
39 Timur Absalyamov, 'Komu on nuzhen etot sport?', *Sobesednik*, 1989, no. 7, p. 11.
40 L. Kedrov, 'Sport v vozraste 6 let: za i protiv', *Sport v SSSR*, 1987, no. 6, p. 27.
41 Vlasov, p. 15.
42 Kedrov, p. 27.
43 'Golf i Tumba', *Nedelya*, 1987, no. 41, p. 13; 'Moscow's first golf club gets into the swing of things', *Soviet Weekly*, 27 November 1988, p. 16.
44 A. Bezruchenko, 'Soviet baseball moves on from first base', *Soviet Weekly*, 30 April 1988, p. 14.
45 'Motogonki', *Pravda*, 18 September 1987, p. 4; see also *Moskovskie novosti*, 1988, no. 43, p. 15.
46 'Bears take a place on the grid', *Soviet Weekly*, 16 December 1989, p. 16.

Trends and transformations

47 O. Dun, 'They're off!', *Soviet Weekly*, 30 April 1988, p. 14.
48 Vladimir Kirilluk, 'Ushu', *Sobesednik*, 1988, no. 46, p. 16.
49 'Sovetsky kulturizm', *Molodoi kommunist*, 1989, no. 4, p. 63.
50 'The corrida is coming to Moscow', *Soviet Weekly*, 6 June 1990, p. 16.
51 'Sweet smell of sport sponsorship', *Soviet Weekly*, 26 November 1988, p. 16.
52 'Khokeisty zhdut razresheniya . . .', *Sovetsky sport*, 29 April 1989, p. 4.
53 'Dasayev goes to Sevilla', *Soviet Weekly*, 5 November 1988, p. 16.
54 Vladimir Kirilluk, 'Enter the new sports supporters', *Soviet Weekly*, 6 May 1989, p. 16.
55 'Professional backup still required', *Soviet Weekly*, 30 September 1989, p. 16.
56 V. Dvortsov, 'Skolko nashi "zvyozdy" dolzhny poluchat?', *Moskovskie novosti*, May 1988, no. 19, p. 15.
57 B. Geskin, 'Emotsii i banknoty', *Sovetsky sport*, 28 August 1988, p. 1.
58 S. Petrov, 'Skolko stoit olimpiyskaya komanda', *Moskovskie novosti*, 1988, no. 39, p. 15.
59 D. Rennick, 'Soviet Olympians compete for preset quota of medals', *Korean Herald*, 27 September 1988, p. 9.
60 D. Gradov, 'Kakie summy vyplatili za chempionstvo nashim khokkeistam?', Argumenty i fakty, 2–8, 1990, p. 8.
61 Anatoly Isayev, 'Lomtik olimpiyskovo piroga', *Sobesednik*, 1989, no. 2, p. 12.
62 A. Druzenko, 'Olimpiyskaya slava', *Moskovskie novosti*, November 1988, p. 15. The one-time world champion swimmer Vladimir Salnikov has contrasted the US total of a million public swimming pools with the Soviet figure of 2,500 (V. Salnikov, 'Vremya nadyozhd', *Argumenty i fakty*, 1989, no. 1, p. 3). Another author makes the point that the USSR has one public swimming pool for 115,000 people, West Germany and Japan have one pool for some 3,500 people, Hungary and Czechoslovakia have one for every 12,500 people (see Alexander Churkin, 'Melko plavayev', *Moskovskie novosti*, 15 January 1989, no. 3, p. 15).

Index